FOOD
GUIDE

RECIPES

Great dishes from the UK's best chefs

THE GOOD FOOD GUIDE

RECIPES

Great dishes from the UK's best chefs

The Good Food Guide: Recipes first published in 2010 by Which? Ltd
This paperback edition first published in 2011 by Peto Place Publishing Ltd
2 Marylebone Road, London, NW1 4DF
Email: editors@thegoodfoodguide.co.uk

Distributed by Littlehampton Book Services Ltd,
Faraday Close, Durrington, Worthing, West Sussex BN13 3RB

British Library Cataloguing in Publication Data
A catalogue record for this book is available from the British Library

ISBN 978 1 84490 126 5

1 3 5 7 9 10 8 6 4 2

Great care should be taken when handling the equipment used in the recipes, with
appropriate protective clothing being worn if necessary. The publisher has tested all
the recipes and made every effort to ensure the information in this book is accurate
and up to date, but does not accept any liability for any injury, loss or damage suffered
as a consequence of relying on the information herein.

Project manager: Emma Callery
Designer: Blânche Williams, Harper–Williams
Photographer: Nikki English
Index: Christine Bernstein
Printed and bound by Charterhouse, Hatfield

Paper: Tauro Offset is a totally chlorine free paper produced using timber from sustainably
managed forests. The mill is ISO14001 certified.

To find out more about The Good Food Guide please go to: **www.thegoodfoodguide.co.uk**

PEFC™
PEFC/16-33-160

Contents

MAINS

JONRAY & PETER SANCHEZ-IGLESIAS   96
Traditional beetroot risotto with pickled fennel, pistachios and iced yogurt

ROBERT THOMPSON   100
Pan-roasted fillet of turbot with gratin of razor clam and tomato and watercress

NATHAN OUTLAW   104
Cornish salt ling, squid and mussel stew

STEPHEN MARKWICK   108
Squid with red wine, orange and fennel

TESSA BRAMLEY   112
Sea bass with mango and crab salsa, potato galette and mint and pea sabayon

WILL HOLLAND   116
Halibut with cauliflower, Morteau sausage, honeycomb, lime and curry

PETER JUKES   120
Baked fillet of wild halibut with pine nuts and bacon

VINEET BHATIA   124
Coastal fish moilee with cashew-tempered rice

ALAN CRAIGIE   128
Pan-fried herring fillets and roes with toasted oatmeal, Savoy cabbage and oven-dried tomatoes

SALLY CLARKE   132
Roasted free-range chicken with soft Parmesan polenta and chestnuts

TRISTAN MASON   136
Roast duck with parsnip and vanilla purée, poached pear and spiced bread

RICHARD CORRIGAN   140
Game bird salad with romesco sauce

FRANCES ATKINS   144
Oven-roasted squab pigeon with oxtail and a chocolate sauce

MICHEL ROUX JR   148
Roast woodcock with grapes and marc

BRYAN WEBB   152
Leg of rabbit with black pudding, Carmarthen ham and mustard sauce

NIGEL HAWORTH   156
Venison carpaccio with mushroom pâté, pickled damsons and hazelnuts

GORDON RAMSAY   160
Roasted loin of venison with braised red cabbage, parsnip chips and parsnip purée

PHILIP HOWARD   164
Herb-crusted saddle of lamb with shallot purée and rosemary

DOMINIC CHAPMAN   168
Oxtail and kidney pie

LAURIE GEAR   172
Slow-roasted rib eye of Dedham Vale beef with oxtail croquettes, wet garlic purée and watercress sauce

MICHAEL NORTH   176
Grilled fillet of aged beef with triple-cooked chips, onion rings, baked tomato and tarragon butter

DESSERTS

We all want our cooking to elicit gasps of admiration, lip smacking and requests for seconds. This book will help nail your reputation as a seriously good cook. It is stuffed with imagination, yet nothing seems pretentious or daft. Freshness and flavour are what the authors are after, and thank goodness for that.

Recipes like Sally Clarke's homely roasted chicken with soft Parmesan polenta and chestnuts and Steve Harris's beetroot soup are easy enough for an absolute beginner. And even Raymond Blanc's sophisticated tomato essence risotto with vegetables or Matthew Tomkinson's warm pistachio sponge cake with rhubarb sorbet, rhubarb compote and vanilla custard are still do-able – and just reading them makes you want to achieve those skills.

All the great chefs are included: Richard Corrigan, Angela Hartnett, Nigel Haworth, Mark Hix, Tom Kitchin, Glynn Purnell, Gordon Ramsay, Ruthie Rogers, Marcus Wareing. You name them, they're here. Most of their restaurants have earned a place in *The Good Food Guide* for many years, and the chefs have learnt what food-loving customers want to eat. The result is a book that every keen cook should buy – a thing of beauty and mouth-watering to read. It is a delight.

I also hope it lives in your kitchen at the risk of gravy splotches, rather than lying in state on the coffee table.

Prue Leith, CBE

Foreword

Introduction

The roots of this recipe book lie as far back as 1951, when the first *Good Food Guide* was published, as a response to the awful food then being served by the catering industry. *The Good Food Guide* has since gone from strength to strength, becoming both a national treasure and the UK's bestselling restaurant bible. For our 60th anniversary, therefore, we wanted to illustrate just how far British cooking has come since the first Guide.

This is not an ad-hoc collection of chefs' recipes, however, nor is it simply a vehicle for big-name chefs. It is a book of great recipes that celebrates the talent to be found today in restaurants and pubs across the country and the great British produce they use.

It has been an exciting journey creating this lavish insight into modern dining, but the trickiest task was undoubtedly the first – to come up with the list of which chefs to include. We chose each chef firstly for the impact they've made on the UK's culinary experience, but we also wanted to ensure that we included chefs and restaurants from around the UK, and a good mix of high-profile stars and up-and-coming chefs. We've also included profiles of the chefs and their restaurants to give you an idea of why they are special, and to encourage you to visit to try out the dishes either before or after you've tried them at home.

From long-established favourites (Shaun Hill and Tessa Bramley) to young guns who have come to prominence in the last five years (Will Holland, Jonray and Peter Sanchez-Iglesias) as well as culinary

> **'This recipe book celebrates the talent found today in restaurants and pubs across the country.'**

giants (Raymond Blanc, Heston Blumenthal and Gordon Ramsay), we then asked each chef to supply a recipe that summed up his/her/their particular philosophy, technique and style. Some gave us a dish they can never take off the menu; others gave us seasonal favourites. But each gave us an exciting, high-quality dish that will test your culinary skill – and, no doubt, impress your friends.

Elizabeth David told the story of Mme Poulard, a hotelier from Normandy 100 years ago, whose omelettes were famous. But, when pressed for her secret ingredient, Mme Poulard replied that it was simply eggs, butter and a hot pan. Here, in a nutshell, is the secret of any successful cook: the best ingredients and the right equipment. Each of these recipes has been thoroughly tested in a domestic kitchen and we've included a glossary of unfamiliar cooking terms and equipment (and where to buy it). We've also tried to retain each chef's individual style in the ingredients and recipes. The rest is up to you!

One of the chefs included in these pages told me he learned to cook by eating top chefs' dishes in their restaurants and then replicating them at home from their cookery books. For anyone looking to up their culinary game, this book is an impressive masterclass.

Elizabeth Carter
Consultant Editor of *The Good Food Guide*

Starters

STEPHEN HARRIS
THE SPORTSMAN

With a history degree and a few years' teaching under his belt, not to mention time as a financial consultant, Stephen Harris is not your typical just-fell-into-it chef. Nor does his restaurant, a weather-beaten old pub overlooking coastal grazing marshes, conform to the dictates of fine dining; expect bare tables, paper napkins and to order at the bar. Yet Harris has created something remarkable with his sophisticated form of no-frills British cooking, establishing The Sportsman as one of the top culinary addresses in the country.

'Working directly with farmers feels natural, using produce that's never been to market.'

From amateur chef ('rather like those people who go on *MasterChef*') to being listed as the Editors' Best Chef of 2010 and one of *The Good Food Guide*'s top 50 restaurants, is the stuff of dreams – and determined spadework. The financial job funded some obsessive eating out and, armed with the cookbooks of such 1990s luminaries as Nico Ladenis and Marco Pierre White, Harris would cook the dishes he had tried in their restaurants. When he eventually sought work as a commis chef, it was to learn how professional kitchens operated – he knew he could cook. Now his food is less about the old fine dining style and more about pure flavours. In such an atmospheric location, with great farms and great produce on the doorstep, Stephen Harris delivers ultra-local food in simple surroundings.

The Sportsman | Faversham Road, Seasalter, Whitstable, Kent CT5 4BP
(01227) 273370 | **www.thesportsmanseasalter.co.uk**

Beetroot soup
Stephen Harris

SERVES 6–8

1 tbsp olive oil or knob of butter
1 red onion, peeled and chopped
Small handful of finely sliced cabbage
450g cooked beetroot, peeled and diced
2 tbsp red wine vinegar
Sea salt
Juice of 1 lime

TO SERVE
Sour cream
Handful of chives, snipped
Lime juice

1 Heat the oil or butter in a large saucepan and then sweat the red onion over a low heat for about 5 minutes or until soft. Add the cabbage and leave to sweat for a further 2–3 minutes or until soft. Add the beetroot and increase the heat.

2 Add the red wine vinegar, bringing it to the boil. Once it has evaporated pour over enough boiling water until the vegetables are just covered – if you add too much water, the soup will be too thin. You can always make a soup thinner later, but you can't thicken it again. Let the soup boil rapidly for 3–4 minutes or until the vegetables are soft.

3 Remove from the heat and purée in a blender, in batches if necessary. Return to the saucepan and adjust the thickness with water if necessary. Add salt and lime juice to taste.

4 To serve, pour the soup into warmed bowls. Place 1 tsp of sour cream in the middle of each and sprinkle over chives, drops of lime juice and salt crystals.

'This is one of my favourite soups. Use water rather than stock so the clarity of the beetroot flavour shines through.'

CHRIS JOHNSON &
ABDULLA NASEEM
RAMSONS

It takes unique qualities to open a restaurant with no formal training and to be listed, 24 years later, not only as one of *The Good Food Guide*'s longest-serving restaurants, but also as one of its top 50 restaurants, with a notable wine list to boot. But, as the Guide noted in 1988: 'Chris Johnson and Ros Hunter share a glorious, eccentric, intense obsession for food and drink.'

Johnson, first with Ros Hunter and now with Abdulla Naseem, has shown a canny ability to move with the times. He has reinvented the former Village Restaurant premises many times over, rejigging the components of wine cellar, deli, coffee bar and restaurant as times have changed. The current set-up consists of a small, elegant ground-floor restaurant, serving pan-Italian food, and the basement Hideaway, modelled on an Italian rural wine shop.

Maldives-born Naseem has headed the kitchen for a decade since Hunter retired in the late 1990s, and his background of French, Italian and Asian cuisine and superb fish cookery skills has been reflected in the changes to the menu. The nettle soup (see overleaf), first created by Hunter and later adapted by Naseem, continues to make its annual seasonal appearance. One thing that has remained constant, however, is the search for first-class seasonal produce, which takes in ingredients both locally sourced and from Italy.

ramsons | 18 Market Place, Ramsbottom, Manchester BL0 9HT
(01706) 825070 | **www.ramsons-restaurant.com**

> '*Food has always been a great interest in my life; I wanted to be a farmer when I was a kid.*'
> *Chris Johnson*

Nettle soup
Chris Johnson & Abdulla Naseem

SERVES 8

4 tbsp extra virgin olive oil

1 large white onion, peeled and sliced

4 garlic cloves (or 100g ramsons –
   wild garlic – leaves), peeled and finely
   chopped, plus flowers, for serving

2 large Maris Piper potatoes, peeled
   and diced

1 celeriac, peeled and diced

1.5 litre chicken (or vegetable) stock

500g young nettle tops (top 6 leaves only)

100g baby spinach

50ml single cream

Sea salt and freshly ground black pepper

FOR THE WILD GARLIC INFUSION

5 wild garlic (ramsons) leaves

50ml extra virgin olive oil

1 Heat the oil in a large saucepan and gently cook the onion and garlic (or ramsons leaves) for about 5 minutes or until soft.
2 Add the potatoes and celeriac and stir for 1 minute. Then add the stock and bring to the boil. Reduce the heat and leave to simmer for 15–20 minutes or until the potatoes and celeriac are soft and cooked through.
3 Remove from the heat and, while it is still hot, use a hand blender to blend the nettles and spinach into the soup.
4 Add the cream and season to taste. Nettles can have a peppery flavour so you probably won't need to add much pepper. Pass the soup through a fine sieve into a clean saucepan.
5 To make the wild garlic infusion, put the wild garlic leaves and olive oil into a blender and whizz to combine. Pass the purée though a fine sieve into a small saucepan and gently warm.
6 Reheat the soup before serving, pour into warmed bowls and top with the wild garlic infusion and a ramsons flower.

'Nettles are an excellent source of vitamins and, way back in the early 1980s, our organic market gardener, George Cooper, actively grew them as companion plants and suggested to Ros that they might make good soup.'

HESTON BLUMENTHAL
THE FAT DUCK

Heston Blumenthal is a one-off. He does not do grand cuisine and he is not an imitator. He opened The Fat Duck in August 1995 after working with, well, hardly anybody. He learned about food by reading *Larousse Gastronomique* from cover to cover and by eating in most of France's top restaurants. His first paid job in a kitchen, however, was in his own – The Fat Duck.

Originally serving classical French dishes (steak and chips with *sauce moelle* and *petit salé* of duck with an especially fine potato purée were highlights in *The Good Food Guide 1997*), this culinary alchemist slowly developed the modern approach to cooking for which he is now famous.

Devotees of The Fat Duck will tell you that the food is not only about meticulous research, culinary know-how or multisensory alchemy, it's also about having fun – just look at the amazing palate cleanser of nitrogen-poached green tea and lime mousse (see overleaf). Today this modest former pub in the well-heeled village of Bray is considered one of the best restaurants in the world, while its chef has scored a perfect ten out of ten in *The Good Food Guide* in 2009, 2010 and 2011.

The Fat Duck | 1 High Street, Bray, Berkshire SL6 2AQ
(01628) 580333 | **www.thefatduck.co.uk**

'Creativity is important to me. In fact, it is central to what I do and my only concern is that there just aren't enough hours in the day.'

Nitro-poached green tea and lime mousse
Heston Blumenthal

MAKES 15 SPOONFULS

FOR THE GREEN TEA SYRUP

200g fructose

16g pectin jaune

30g green tea

2 limes, zest removed with a peeler

4g salt

FOR THE GREEN TEA AND LIME MOUSSE

187g lime juice

Caster sugar (optional)

50ml vodka

2g green tea powder

110g egg whites

2g malic acid

TO SERVE

Green tea powder

Specific equipment: see page 259

1 To make the green tea syrup, bring 1 litre of water to the boil in a large saucepan. Sieve the fructose and the pectin together into a bowl and whisk into the boiling water and bring back to the boil, whisking continuously. Simmer for a further 5 minutes, still whisking continuously. Chill the mixture over ice to 4°C. When cool, add the green tea, lime zest and salt and allow to infuse for 2 hours. Pass through muslin and weigh out 650g.

2 Before making the green tea and lime mousse, you may wish to pasteurise the lime juice. Combine it with 10 per cent of its weight in caster sugar and seal in a sous vide bag at full pressure. Place the bag in a water bath set at 70°C for 10 minutes, then cool rapidly in an ice bath.

3 For the mousse, mix a little of the vodka with all the green tea powder to form a paste, then add the remaining vodka. Mix the vodka and green tea in a bowl with the 650g of green tea syrup, the lime juice, egg whites and malic acid and blitz with a hand-held electric mixer for 15 seconds to ensure that all the ingredients are thoroughly incorporated. Pour this into a cream whipper charged with two cream charges, or whisk with a hand-held electric mixer until the cream is white and foamy.

4 To serve, discharge a spoonful of the mousse onto a dessert spoon and drop the mousse from the spoon into liquid nitrogen which, at 197°C below freezing, will instantly and still very gently freeze the ingredients. Leave for 10 seconds before carefully turning over. Leave for a further 10 seconds before removing from the nitrogen extremely carefully.

5 Place the mousse on a plate, dusted with green tea powder, and serve immediately as a palate cleanser.

'I really dislike the taste of toothpaste in my mouth before dining. So I created this dish in 2001 as a way to prepare and cleanse the palate, but still excite the mouth and whet the appetite for what is to follow.'

ROWLEY LEIGH
LE CAFÉ ANGLAIS

The famously irrepressible Rowley Leigh is surprisingly modest when it comes to acknowledging his role in the British culinary revolution of the 1980s. He maintains that he isn't quite sure whether he was a prophet leading us out of the wilderness or more 'a sort of King Canute'. In fact, there is no debate about it. He was a prime mover in a phenomenon *The Good Food Guide* identified at the time as 'modern British cooking'.

Not to be confused with the parallel return of traditional domestic cookery (the fish cakes and rice pudding tendency), modern British cooking was a mix-and-match style that happily drew on influences from all over the known world while still respecting their integrity. Leigh says: 'If the French did Thai food, it would be a French version of Thai, whereas we wanted it to speak for itself.' Coupled with a move to large-scale restaurants (prior to Le Café Anglais, Rowley Leigh's home for two decades was Kensington Place), great cooking was all of a sudden prised out of the haute cuisine context of hushed formal reverence.

Some things have come full circle. Having banished those kidney-shaped side plates of vegetables ('like hospital food') and integrated them into the main dish, Leigh now confesses to a recovered preference for a more traditional, if pared-down, style. Meanwhile, the DIY element, such as dunking anchovy toast into Parmesan custard (see overleaf), is all part of the fun.

Le Café Anglais | 8 Porchester Gardens, Notting Hill, London W2 4DB
(020) 7221 1415 | **www.lecafeanglais.co.uk**

Parmesan custard and anchovy toast
Rowley Leigh

MAKES 4 INDIVIDUAL CUSTARDS

150ml single cream
150ml milk
50g Parmesan cheese, finely grated
2 egg yolks
Salt and white pepper
Pinch of cayenne pepper
6 anchovy fillets
25g unsalted butter, softened
4 very thin slices of *pain de campagne*

Specific equipment: see page 259

1 Mix the cream, milk and all but 1 tbsp of the cheese in a bowl and then warm the mixture gently over a pan of boiling water until the cheese has melted.

2 Allow to cool completely and then whisk in the egg yolks together with a pinch of salt, some finely milled white pepper and a little cayenne.

3 Preheat the oven to 150°C/Gas 2 and lightly butter the china moulds or ramekins.

4 Pour the custard into four 80ml china moulds or ramekins and place them in a pan of boiling water. Cover with buttered greaseproof paper and bake in the oven for 20–30 minutes or until the mixture has just set.

5 Meanwhile, mash the anchovies and butter to a smooth paste and spread over 2 of the slices of bread. Cover with the remaining bread and toast in a sandwich maker or panini machine.

6 Preheat the grill to hot. Sprinkle the remaining Parmesan cheese over the warm custards and brown gently under the grill. Cut the toasted anchovy sandwiches into little fingers and serve alongside the custards.

'I hate the term, but this has become a "signature dish" at the Café. It helps that both anchovies and Parmesan are two of my favourite ingredients.'

MARCUS WAREING
MARCUS WAREING AT THE BERKELEY

Marcus Wareing has well and truly drawn a line beneath his restaurant's former incarnation as Pétrus, and it's all down to quiet determination and accomplished cooking. Wareing is, without doubt, one of the most brilliant chefs working in Britain today with a back story that glitters with former spells at the Savoy, Le Gavroche, Aubergine and L'Oranger in the UK, and with Daniel Boulud in New York and Guy Savoy in Paris.

Wareing was born in Lancashire, the son of a fruit and potato merchant who taught him the importance of great-quality produce, and, with a brother already in the business, becoming a chef 'seemed the natural road to take'. Wareing's cooking is all about fine ingredients — be

'The people around me are the driving force of my cooking. Without them I would be in a completely different position.'

it a lobe of foie gras, a crunchy organic carrot or a juicy vine tomato — and how he can bring out the very best in each to enhance their natural greatness.

Wareing not only excels at interesting texture and contrasts in flavour, but also displays skill at embracing the most technical elements of cooking while presenting dishes in a beautiful yet unpretentious way. Dining at his restaurant, a glorious synthesis of the traditional and the modern, is a truly memorable experience.

Marcus Wareing at the Berkeley | The Berkeley, Wilton Place, Belgravia, London SW1X 7RL
(020) 7235 1200 | **www.marcus-wareing.com**

Marinated vine tomatoes with ricotta, aged balsamic vinegar and croutes
Marcus Wareing

SERVES 4

500g cherry vine tomatoes
12 slices of rye bread, cut very finely
Olive oil, for cooking
90g ricotta cheese
Aged balsamic vinegar, for drizzling
Celery cress, to garnish

FOR THE MARINADE
15g tomato purée
Small handful of thyme
1 bay leaf
3 garlic cloves, peeled and chopped
2 tsp caster sugar
½ tsp salt
Good pinch of saffron
25ml balsamic vinegar
Olive oil, to cover the tomatoes

1 Bring a large saucepan of water to the boil and blanch the tomatoes in small batches in the water for 1–2 minutes. Transfer them to a bowl of cold water with a slotted spoon and then peel. Prick all over with the point of a sharp knife and put into another bowl.
2 For the marinade, place all the ingredients in a small saucepan and heat gently. Whisk together and then pour over the tomatoes so they are all covered. Cover with cling film and leave in a warm place for 12 hours. Then refrigerate for at least 12 hours.
3 When ready to serve, preheat the oven to 180°C/Gas 4. To make the croutes, brush the bread with olive oil on both sides and bake in the oven for about 5 minutes or until golden.
4 Divide the tomatoes between 4 bowls and add small spoonfuls of the ricotta and the croutes. Drizzle over the aged balsamic vinegar and garnish with the celery cress.

'This is all about making the tomato taste amazing. It's a dish that is so basic, yet so wonderful if all the elements are right.'

RAYMOND BLANC
LE MANOIR AUX QUAT'SAISONS

Where does culinary greatness originate? For most, a prolonged apprenticeship in several of the world's important kitchens, after qualifying from college, is a must. Then there are those for whom innate self-belief is enough. When the young Raymond Blanc and his wife Jenny pooled all their resources to open the small Les Quat'Saisons in Oxford in the recession-bound 1970s, self-belief was the only thing holding up a chef who had never had a cookery lesson in his life.

However, by the time Blanc opened Le Manoir aux Quat'Saisons in 1984, he had become one of a generation of culinary superstars and has been listed in *The Good Food Guide* ever since. With its extensive kitchen gardens and unruffled tranquillity, Le Manoir remains a destination restaurant. Blanc's style has acquired the burnish of experience, but his creativity seems inexhaustible and he has never lost the enthusiasm for fine ingredients that can make something as simple as a summer vegetable risotto (see overleaf) into a thing of beauty.

Lifetime achievement award
To mark the 60th anniversary of *The Good Food Guide*, the 2011 edition includes a special lifetime achievement award presented to Raymond Blanc in recognition of his unerring commitment to consistency, quality and seasonal produce. It has been 32 years since the overnight success of Les Quat'Saisons, three decades that have earned Blanc a reputation as a culinary giant. Few chefs can show such dedication and consistency or such an uncanny ability to read the mood of the times.

Le Manoir aux Quat'Saisons | Church Road, Great Milton, Oxfordshire OX44 7PD
(01844) 278881 | **www.manoir.com**

'It is just cooking. There is no fast food or cheating. I like to show how the creative process of cooking can be so rewarding.'

Tomato essence risotto with summer vegetables
Raymond Blanc

SERVES 4

FOR THE TOMATO ESSENCE

1.25kg cherry tomatoes

½ celery stick, finely chopped

½ shallot, peeled and finely chopped

¼ fennel bulb, finely chopped

½ garlic clove, peeled and sliced

Small sprig of thyme, leaves removed and chopped

10g basil leaves, chopped

2 tsp sea salt

Pinch of cayenne pepper

4 drops of Tabasco sauce

FOR THE RISOTTO

¼ onion, peeled and finely chopped

½ garlic clove, peeled and puréed

2 tbsp extra virgin olive oil

200g carnaroli rice

4 pinches of sea salt

2 pinches of white pepper

150g butternut squash, cut into 1cm dice

1 baby fennel bulb, sliced

2 baby courgettes, halved lengthways and sliced into 1cm pieces

4 baby asparagus spears, cut into 1cm lengths

80g shelled peas

½ tsp coriander seeds, lightly crushed

4 tsp finely grated Parmesan cheese

2 tbsp mascarpone cheese, plus extra for serving

10 cherry tomatoes

4 black olives

TO SERVE

Scattering of pine nuts and herbs

1 If possible, make the tomato essence the day before you need it to allow the flavour to develop fully. Put all the ingredients for the essence into a food processor and blitz three times for 2 seconds each, using the pulse button. Do not over-blitz the tomatoes as the skins then break down, resulting in a completely different, coarser flavour. Correctly made, the essence should be a pale golden colour.

2 Leave the tomato mixture to marinate for a minimum of 3 hours during which time the salt will draw out the juices from the tomatoes and bring about a wonderful exchange of flavours between the herbs and the vegetables.

3 Transfer to a double-folded muslin cloth and hang it over a saucepan to collect the liquid overnight. This recipe will give you more than enough essence to make the risotto, but it is the minimum weight needed to extract the most juice from the tomatoes. Reserve the tomato pulp to make a soup, to use as a sauce for pasta or in a chicken casserole.

4 To cook the risotto, bring 300ml of water to the boil in a saucepan. In a separate pan, sweat the onion and garlic in the olive oil on a low heat for 2 minutes or until soft. Stir in the rice and continue to cook, on a medium heat, for 2 minutes or until the grains of rice appear shiny. Season with the salt and pepper. Add the butternut squash, stir in the hot water and bring to a gentle simmer.

5 Heat 300ml of the tomato essence in a separate pan and then add to the rice and butternut squash. Simmer very gently and after 20 minutes add the fennel, courgettes, asparagus, peas and coriander seeds. Continue to cook for about 5 minutes more or until the rice is al dente. If the rice gets too dry, top up with hot water.

6 Add the Parmesan and mascarpone cheeses, tomatoes and olives. Taste, adjust the seasoning if necessary and serve in 4 warmed bowls with a dollop of mascarpone cheese on top and scattered with the pine nuts (toasted in a medium oven for 10 minutes, if you wish) and herbs. In the restaurant, we like to add some pesto sauce to garnish the tomatoes.

'This is one of my favourite dishes.
It is perfect for the summer when
tomatoes are at their best.'

SIMON ROGAN
L'ENCLUME

It was a brave move to open a restaurant focusing on tasting menus of some seven to twenty small courses in a part of the country where fine dining usually means a country house hotel with a repertoire set in stone. It made quite a splash in the Lake District. Eight years on, however, and Simon Rogan is now considered one of the most innovative chefs in Britain, with L'Enclume as the Lakes' chief culinary attraction.

Early influences such as Marco Pierre White and Jean-Christophe Novelli have been enhanced by the French greats – Alain Senderens, Marc Veyrat and Pierre Gagnaire – who pointed Rogan in the direction he now follows. While he

'I am really excited about the ability to pull an item out of the ground to our specification, to be used within hours and without seeing the inside of the fridge.'

maintains an interest in technology and new concepts, the focus for his restaurant, housed in a former smithy in a narrow street near Cartmel Priory, is its connection to its surroundings, Cumbria's larder. Foraging is important for Rogan, while the purchase of nearby Howbarrow Organic Farm has allowed him to produce food to his own requirements, resulting in a very natural and healthy style of eating.

L'Enclume I Cavendish Street, Cartmel, Cumbria LA11 6PZ
(015395) 36362 I **www.lenclume.co.uk**

Deep-fried polenta mushroom balls with smoked eel and sweetcorn purée

Simon Rogan

SERVES 4

FOR THE SWEETCORN PURÉE
250g sweetcorn kernels
25ml chicken stock
Salt and freshly ground black pepper

FOR THE MUSHROOM BALLS
150g cream cheese
1 tbsp chopped alexanders or celery
24 cup mushrooms, about 3cm in diameter
Plain flour, for coating
2 eggs, beaten
2 tbsp caraway seeds
70g polenta
Vegetable oil, for deep-frying

TO SERVE
100g smoked eel, cut into 3cm dice
Few sprigs of dill
Chive, garlic, campanula and alexander flowers
Extra virgin rapeseed oil
Unrefined sea salt

1 To make the sweetcorn purée, blanch the sweetcorn kernels in boiling salted water, strain and then liquidise with the chicken stock until smooth. Put through a fine sieve into a clean saucepan and season to taste with salt and pepper. Keep warm.

2 For the mushroom balls, first combine the cream cheese and alexanders or celery with seasoning in a bowl.

3 Remove the mushroom stems and trim a little off the inside to make more room for the cream cheese. Then divide the cream cheese mix between 12 of the mushrooms. Sandwich with the other 12 mushrooms to form balls.

4 Put the flour on a plate, the eggs in a bowl and then mix the caraway seeds with the polenta on another plate. Dip the mushroom balls first in the flour, then in the egg and finally the polenta mix.

5 Heat the vegetable oil to 170°C in a saucepan and fry the mushroom balls for about 30 seconds or until golden.

6 To serve, place swishes of the sweetcorn purée on 4 warmed plates. Arrange 4 pieces of the diced smoked eel next to 3 mushroom balls and garnish with the sprigs of dill and flowers. Finish by drizzling with rapeseed oil and sprinkling sea salt over the plates.

'This dish was devised for the home cook, but gives some insight into the philosophy of L'Enclume – a mixture of wild and organic farm produce sitting side by side in harmony. Light and balanced, it is also full of flavour.'

'Over the years, I have become more practical and have greater awareness of – and more interest in – where the ingredients come from.'

MARK HIX
HIX OYSTER & FISH HOUSE

Whether it was fishing in Dorset as a kid or picking tomatoes from his grandfather's greenhouse, seasonal food played a big part in Mark Hix's life from an early age. Having chosen home economics over metalwork at school – 'because I didn't know what I wanted to do when I left' – he attended Weymouth College and completed his City & Guilds in catering. After a short spell as commis chef at the Hilton, Hix then moved to the Grosvenor House Hotel where he worked for Anton Edelmann before working under Anton Mosimann at the Dorchester. No mean training for someone who didn't know what he wanted to do when he left school.

At the age of just 22, Hix got his big break when he got his first head chef position at The Candlewick Room. Only five years later he became executive head chef for Caprice Holdings, overseeing eight restaurants, including The Ivy and Scott's in Mayfair. After 17 years with the group, Hix knew it was time to concentrate on his own projects and so, in 2008, he opened his Hix Oyster & Chop House in Smithfield, closely followed by Hix Oyster & Fish House overlooking Lyme Bay and then Hix in Soho in 2009.

An ambassador for British cooking, seasonal produce and wild food, he says he can now 'pass my experience and knowledge on to the customers and chefs that work for me'. Yet, despite building something of a restaurant empire of his own, he says his real passion is still 'finding new producers, discovering new dishes and meeting interesting people'.

Hix Oyster & Fish House I Cobb Road, Lyme Regis, Dorset DT7 3JP
(01297) 446910 I **www.restaurantsetcltd.co.uk**

Fried duck's egg with sprue asparagus and brown shrimps

Mark Hix

SERVES 4

250g sprue or extra-fine asparagus

Salt and freshly ground black pepper

1 tbsp olive oil

4 duck eggs

50g brown shrimps or a tub of potted shrimps

2 good knobs of butter, if using brown shrimps

1 Cut the woody ends from the asparagus and cut the rest of the spears in half if they are long. Cook them in boiling salted water for 3–4 minutes or until tender, and then drain.

2 Heat the olive oil in a frying pan and lightly fry the eggs.

3 Meanwhile, if using brown shrimps, melt the butter in a saucepan and add the shrimps and asparagus. Or place the potted shrimps in a pan and add the asparagus. Season and heat for 1–2 minutes or until hot.

4 Transfer the eggs onto warmed plates and spoon over the asparagus, shrimps and butter. Serve immediately.

'The dish works because it is simple and very few people feature a fried egg on the menu other than for breakfast.'

CHRIS & JEFF GALVIN
GALVIN BISTROT DE LUXE

Two of the most affable chefs on the London restaurant scene, the Galvin brothers climbed the career ladder with hard work and unrivalled determination. They have impeccable pedigrees: big brother Chris (the elder by 11 years and to the right in the photograph above) made a splash as chef-patron of Orrery and overseeing the launch of Almeida for Conran Restaurants before moving on to become executive chef at the Wolseley, while Jeff honed his craft under the kind of chefs that get you noticed, namely Nico Ladenis and Marco Pierre White. When they pooled their talents in 2006 to open the Galvin Bistrot de Luxe in Baker Street, serving traditional French cuisine at affordable prices, everyone wondered why it had taken them so long.

'I was taken to France when I was seven and was hooked on the way of life. At 15 I bought Guérard's book Cuisine Gourmande and had to be a chef.' Chris Galvin

Chris also doubles as the chef-patron of Galvin at Windows, located on the 28th floor of the Hilton Hotel, and, with the opening of Galvin La Chapelle in Spitalfields in late 2009, the brothers seem set on building a mini empire. Lasagne of crab (see overleaf) comes from Jeff's days working with Nico Ladenis and pretty much encapsulates both brothers' skill at upholding the best of traditions while producing superlative modern French cuisine.

Galvin Bistrot de Luxe | 66 Baker Street, Marylebone, London W1U 7DJ
(020) 7935 4007 | **www.galvinrestaurants.com**

Lasagne of Dorset crab and scallops
Chris & Jeff Galvin

MAKES 4 INDIVIDUAL LASAGNES

FOR THE PASTA
140g strong flour
1 egg
1½ egg yolks
½ tbsp olive oil
Salt

FOR THE SCALLOP AND CRAB MOUSSE
150g scallops, white flesh only
150ml double cream
Pinch of cayenne pepper
275g white crab meat

FOR THE SAUCE
1 shallot, peeled and finely diced
200g unsalted butter, diced
50ml white wine
25ml white wine vinegar
50ml chicken stock
25ml double cream

TO SERVE
2 tbsp finely chopped coriander

Specific equipment: see page 259

1 To make the pasta, place all the ingredients and a pinch of salt into a food processor and blitz until they resemble breadcrumbs. Remove to a floured worktop and knead for about 5 minutes to make a dough. Wrap in cling film and place in the fridge for at least an hour. When rested, roll out using a pasta machine until very thin. You will have much more than you need, so save the rest for another dish.

2 Bring a saucepan of salted water to the boil and cover 2 baking trays with cling film. Blanch 3 sheets of the pasta in the water for 1 minute and then plunge into iced water. When cold, drain off the water and use a 6cm-diameter metal ring to cut 12 circles from the lasagne. Lay them on the prepared trays.

3 For the scallop and crab mousse, place the bowl of a food processor into the freezer for 1 hour to chill. Return the bowl to the processor and add the scallop flesh. Blitz for 3–4 minutes or until it has nicely puréed then slowly add the double cream and season with salt and cayenne pepper. Fold in the white crab meat.

4 To make the sauce, cook the diced shallot in a little of the butter for about 3 minutes on a medium heat until soft but not browned. Add the white wine, white wine vinegar and 50ml of water. Bring to the boil, reduce to a syrup and then add the chicken stock. Reduce to a syrup again and then add the double cream. Boil for 1 minute and then slowly add the rest of the butter, maintaining the heat in the sauce as you go. Check the seasoning and keep warm.

5 To make each lasagne, place four 6cm-diameter x 4.5cm-deep metal rings in a steamer pan. Then place a disc of pasta in the bottom of each. Half fill with the scallop and crab mousse and add a second pasta disc. Fill the ring with mousse and top with a third disc. Steam the lasagnes for 12 minutes or until cooked through.

6 Place each lasagne ring in a warmed bowl and run a small knife between the ring and the lasagne to remove the ring. Add half of the chopped coriander to the sauce and spoon 3 tbsp into each bowl. Scatter the remaining coriander over the lasagnes and serve immediately.

'We use only hand-picked Dorset crab for this lasagne and have had letters of protest when we tried to remove it from the menu!'

ANGELA HARTNETT
MURANO

If there were awards for sheer indefatigability, with special commendations for not resting on one's laurels, Angela Hartnett — for many, Britain's premier female chef — would be first in line. Her trajectory over the past decade has been remarkable, taking her from the launch of Amaryllis in Scotland in 2001 to a stint in the kitchens of the Connaught Hotel, and then, via Dubai and Miami, back to London and her present twin billets at the suave Murano in Mayfair and the York & Albany, on the edge of Regent's Park. Writing cookery books and appearing on TV are what she does in her spare time.

A protégée of the Gordon Ramsay stable, Hartnett's career reflects both the formidable work rate and the commitment to excellence of Ramsay himself. But, more than that, she has carved out her own unmistakable culinary identity. Turning the dining rooms of an austere old stager like the Connaught into a place where inventive, light-footed cooking of great excitement could be found was one of the more noteworthy London accomplishments of recent years, and her Mediterranean-inspired style is now on display within distinctly more contemporary surroundings. Murano hand-blown light fittings and elaborate sculpted chandeliers add to the handsome decor.

There is an underlying simplicity, but also great craft, to her best dishes, which extends from the much-favoured Sunday roasts at the York & Albany to one of the defining restaurant dishes from Murano, scallops with an earthy pumpkin purée (see overleaf).

Murano | 20–22 Queen Street, Mayfair, London W1J 5PP
(020) 7592 1222 | **www.gordonramsay.com**

'I'm often held up to be one of Britain's few women chefs, but the truth is more and more are working just beneath the radar. They may not have the profile yet, but the industry is definitely changing.'

Scallops with pumpkin purée and candied walnuts
Angela Hartnett

SERVES 4

FOR THE APPLE VINAIGRETTE
500ml apple juice
250ml extra virgin olive oil
2 tbsp cider vinegar
Sea salt

FOR THE PUMPKIN PURÉE
500g diced pumpkin
25g chilled butter, plus a little extra, diced
Salt and freshly ground black pepper

FOR THE CANDIED WALNUTS
100g shelled walnuts
200g caster sugar
25g chilled butter, diced

FOR THE SHALLOT CHUTNEY
3 shallots, peeled and very finely diced
100ml Chardonnay or white wine vinegar
Sprig of thyme
1 bay leaf

FOR THE APPLE SALSA
1 Granny Smith apple
½ cucumber
Small handful of chervil, chopped

FOR THE SCALLOPS
2 tsp mild curry powder
8 large scallops
Olive oil, for frying

TO SERVE
4 slices of pata negra ham
Handful of mixed cress

1 To make the apple vinaigrette, pour the apple juice into a large saucepan and bring to the boil. Cook until the juice has reduced to 50ml. Pour it into a bowl, leave to cool and mix with the olive oil and vinegar and a pinch of the sea salt.

2 Next make the pumpkin purée. Tip the diced pumpkin into a separate pan with the 25g of the butter and some salt. Cover with a lid and leave to sweat over a medium heat, stirring occasionally, for about 15 minutes or until the pumpkin starts to release its juices.

3 Remove the lid and continue to cook over a medium heat for 10–15 minutes or until the pumpkin flesh is soft and any liquid has evaporated. Transfer to a food processor and blend with a few extra knobs of chilled butter until smooth. Pass the purée through a fine sieve into a bowl and check for seasoning.

4 For the candied walnuts, preheat the oven to 200°C/Gas 6. Scatter the walnuts over a baking sheet in an even layer, then toast in the oven for 2 minutes or until hot.

5 Meanwhile, melt the sugar with 4 tbsp of water in a heavy-based frying pan over a low heat. Once all the sugar has dissolved, increase the heat and cook the sugar to a golden caramel.

6 Carefully add the walnuts to the caramel with a pinch of salt and the diced butter. Swirl the pan about to mix together for a few seconds, then transfer the nuts with a slotted spoon onto a baking sheet lined with baking parchment. Allow the walnuts to cool completely and then roughly chop.

7 For the chutney, add the shallots to a heavy-based pan. Cover with the vinegar and add some salt and the thyme and bay leaf. Cook over a low heat for about 8 minutes or until the liquid has evaporated and the shallots are very soft. Remove the bay leaf.

8 When you are ready to serve, peel, core and cut the apple into 5mm dice and also peel, deseed and cut the cucumber into 5mm dice. Mix the dice with a spoonful of the shallot chutney, the chopped candied walnuts, chervil and vinaigrette.

9 For the scallops, mix together the curry powder and 2 tsp of sea salt in a bowl. Cut the scallops in half horizontally through the middle. Sprinkle both sides of each half with some of the curry powder and salt mix. Heat a little olive oil in a large, non-stick frying pan. Add the scallops and cook on each side for 30–40 seconds or until golden, turning them in the order they were put in. Remove from the pan and leave to rest for a minute.

10 To serve, arrange small spoonfuls of the pumpkin purée around 4 warmed plates and sit the scallop halves on top. Spoon the apple salsa over and around the scallops and add slices of the pata negra ham and the cress on the top.

'This dish is all about contrasts – the softness of the scallops is balanced by the bite of the apple salsa, while the saltiness of the ham is offset by the sweetness of the walnuts.'

DANIEL CLIFFORD
MIDSUMMER HOUSE

It was a spell in a hotel kitchen as a schoolboy on work experience that encouraged Daniel Clifford to become a chef. By his own admission 'not good at school', it was the first time he had had a report with the word 'excellent' in it. Then a stint in France working for the two-Michelin-starred chef Jean Bardet made an early impression on Clifford. A high-scoring fixture in *The Good Food Guide* since the 2000 edition, he is very much at home in this well-maintained Victorian villa on the bank of the Cam overlooking Midsummer Common.

Considered to be part of that elite band of British chefs that has pushed back the boundaries of French-centred haute cuisine, Clifford has now reappraised his style, noting, 'I didn't start cooking to make jellies and foams'. He has, to some extent, simplified his dishes, going back to those basic skills learnt when training, and letting the fantastic produce he loves speak for itself. His scallop dish (see overleaf) is part of that culinary background, described in the Guide as a 'beguiling, intelligent and precise' balance of flavours.

'There's no need for luxury ingredients all the time. A piece of pollack is as good as a piece of turbot if cooked the right way.'

Midsummer House | Midsummer Common, Cambridge, Cambridgeshire CB4 1HA
(01223) 369299 | **www.midsummerhouse.co.uk**

Seared scallops, celeriac and truffle purée and apple jelly
Daniel Clifford

SERVES 6

FOR THE APPLE JELLY
500ml apple juice
200ml Granny Smith apple juice
10g carrageen or gelatine
Salt
Pinch of caster sugar

FOR THE CELERIAC AND TRUFFLE PURÉE
250g celeriac, peeled and chopped
200ml milk
100ml double cream
Lemon juice
1cm black truffle, chopped
20ml white truffle oil

FOR THE SCALLOPS
12 extra-large scallops
Olive oil, for frying
Sea salt

TO SERVE
3 Granny Smith apples
Lemon juice
Black truffle, finely sliced

1 Make the apple jelly in advance of cooking the celeriac and scallops. Put the apple juices into a large saucepan and bring to the boil. Turn down the heat and let the juice reduce by two thirds (about 10 minutes).

2 Pass the juice through a chinois or sieve and leave it for about 10 minutes to cool. Then strain the juice through muslin into a saucepan and mix in the carrageen or gelatine. Season with salt and sugar to taste and bring the mixture to the boil, stirring occasionally. Pass through a chinois or fine sieve one more time and leave to set, which will take about 2 hours. When the jelly is set, dice into small cubes to serve.

3 To make the celeriac and truffle purée, boil the celeriac in the milk together with 200ml of water for about 20 minutes or until soft. In a separate pan, bring the cream to the boil and set aside. Drain the liquid from the celeriac and transfer the celeriac and cream to a food processor. Blend until it is smooth. Season the purée with salt and lemon juice to taste and then leave it on a low heat to keep warm while you cook the scallops.

4 For the scallops, preheat the oven to 190°C/Gas 5. Add a little olive oil to a hot, ovenproof frying pan. Season the scallops with sea salt and then place them in the pan. Sear on a high heat for about 30 seconds on each side or until golden, then place in the oven for 1 minute to finish cooking.

5 To serve, cut the apples into matchsticks, keeping the skin on. Mix the chopped truffle and truffle oil into the celeriac purée and place a spoonful onto each one of 6 warmed plates. Add the scallops, sprinkle over sea salt and a squeeze of lemon juice and top with the chopped apple and black truffle. Put a few cubes of the apple jelly near to one of the scallops. In the restaurant, we also like to add some apple caramel to garnish the plate. Serve immediately.

'The scallop dish has been on the menu since day one, but it has evolved and evolved. Now I can't take it off the menu!'

SHAUN RANKIN
BOHEMIA

This Yorkshire-born chef grew up with an interest in cooking, encouraged by his mum, who used to tell him stories about the smallholding where her parents kept pigs and chickens. Shaun Rankin remembers his grandmother's tattered old recipe book and uses her ham hock soup recipe to this day.

While this early experience encouraged a feel for raw ingredients, it was jobs in London, Chicago and Sydney that gave Rankin the experience to excel at his craft — and then he lost his heart to Jersey when working as sous chef at Longueville Manor. Since taking over Bohemia (part of the ultra-chic Club Hotel & Spa at the heart of St Helier's financial quarter) in 2003, he has never looked back, flying the Jersey flag for his adopted home with classically based but unmistakably modern cooking that does more than its bit for local suppliers and seasonal foods. As the recipe for scallop ravioli reveals (see overleaf), Rankin often uses classic themes as the jumping-off point for startling and innovative ideas. In the words of *The Good Food Guide 2011*, 'the cooking capitalises on Jersey's best products and is hardly ever short of brilliant.'

Bohemia | Green Street, St Helier, Jersey JE2 4UH
(01534) 872809 | **www.bohemiajersey.com**

'I can't stress enough how fantastic the local produce is here – I'm a huge advocate of Jersey asparagus, potatoes, oysters and hand-dived scallops, to name but a few.'

Ravioli of Jersey scallop with crab, scallop and sweetcorn velouté, buttered lobster and basil

Shaun Rankin

SERVES 8

FOR THE PASTA
250g 00 flour
Salt
1 tbsp olive oil
1½ eggs
4 egg yolks

FOR THE SCALLOP MOUSSE
450g scallops, reserving 8 scallops
  to garnish
1 egg white (optional)
85ml whipping cream
Salt and white pepper
Splash of Noilly Prat (vermouth)

**FOR THE SCALLOP AND
SWEETCORN VELOUTÉ**
½ corn on the cob
600g scallop skirts
½ banana shallot, peeled and finely
  sliced
½ garlic clove, peeled and crushed
Small sprig of thyme
1 bay leaf
35ml Noilly Prat (vermouth)
65ml white wine
235ml whipping cream
235ml double cream
Squeeze of lemon juice

FOR THE LOBSTER
2 lobsters
1 carrot, peeled and chopped
1 leek, trimmed and chopped

4 shallots, peeled and chopped
Small handful of parsley stalks
5 black peppercorns
1 bay leaf
100g butter

FOR THE CRAB
1 chancre (Cromer) crab
Juice of ½ lemon
Handful of parsley stalks

TO FINISH
Lemon juice
Micro basil or shredded basil
  leaves

Specific equipment: see page 259

1 To make the pasta, sift the flour into a food processor. Start to mix the flour, adding a pinch of salt and the oil. Mix for 1 minute and then slowly add the eggs and egg yolks. Before adding the last egg, check the dough is pliable and firm to soft and only add it if it's not. Place the dough on a floured worktop and knead for 5 minutes by stretching and folding the dough. Wrap the dough in cling film and refrigerate for at least 30 minutes.

2 For the mousse, chill a food processor bowl, blade and lid for 30 minutes in the freezer. Add the scallop meat with a good pinch of salt to the processor and blend for 1 minute or until smooth. Scrape the sides of the bowl down and blend for a few more minutes.

3 Add the egg white (this is only required if the scallops are a few days old) to the scallop meat and blend for 1 minute more and then pass through a fine drum sieve into a bowl. Sit the bowl over a pan of iced water and allow to rest in the fridge for 20 minutes.

4 Using a spatula, work in some of the cream by stretching and folding the scallop meat around the bowl. Then add the rest of the cream, little by little, over four or five 20-minute intervals, allowing the mousse to rest each time in the fridge. It is important not to add too much cream as the mousse will become too soft (you can always add more after the next stage if needed). When enough cream has been worked in, give the mousse a good beat. It should now be looking glossy. Season with salt and white pepper and the Noilly Prat.

5 Tightly wrap 1 tbsp of mousse in cling film. Tie both ends and lightly poach in simmering water for 5 minutes. The mousse should be soft but firm. If it is too firm, it will need more cream. If it is chewy, it will need another good beat. Adjust the cream or beat further, if necessary, and try again. Once happy with the consistency, repeat with the remaining mixture. Refrigerate until ready to use.

6 To make the scallop ravioli, using a pasta machine roll out the pasta dough until you get to the thinnest setting. Using a 7cm-diameter cutter, cut out 16 discs. Keep covered on the worktop with cling film so they don't dry out. Spoon a little of the mousse into the middle of 8 discs. Wet the rim of each disk with cold water and place the other disc on top. Place a 6cm-diameter cutter over the top to shape the ravioli and then remove the cutter. Cook the ravioli in simmering salted water for 3 minutes, then refresh in iced water. Reserve.

7 To make the velouté, place the corn on the cob in boiling salted water and cook for 8–12 minutes or until tender. Strip the kernels off the cob and set aside.

8 Heat a large saucepan until very hot. Add the scallop skirts, shallot, garlic and herbs, stirring vigorously until the scallops' moisture has been released. Add the Noilly Prat and reduce by two thirds. Then add the wine and reduce by two thirds again. Add both types of cream and bring to the boil. Cook for 2 minutes and pass through a sieve. Squeeze all the liquid from the scallop skirts, discard the liquid and return the scallop to the sauce. Add seasoning and lemon juice, then put aside.

9 Freeze the lobsters for 10–15 minutes. Pull the heads away from the bodies, break off the claws and remove the tails. Tie each tail to a heatproof knife to keep it straight. Fill a large saucepan with water and add the vegetables. Add the parsley, peppercorns and bay leaf, bring to the boil, reduce the heat and let simmer. Cook the claws for 7 minutes, adding the tails after 3 minutes, and then put into iced water. Crack the meat out of the claws, dice and refrigerate. Place the tails in a sous vide bag with the butter, then seal and refrigerate.

10 Place the crab in a large saucepan and cover with cold water. Add the lemon juice and parsley stalks and bring to the boil. Refresh in cold water and then remove the claws and crack the shells. Remove the crabmeat from the claws and refrigerate all the meat until needed.

11 Place the bag with the lobster tails in hot water to warm through and put the ravioli in a pan of simmering water for 4 minutes. Heat the velouté, add the reserved 8 scallops and poach for 2 minutes. Add seasoning, some lemon juice, the crabmeat and sweetcorn kernels. Cut the lobster tails into 8 medallions. To serve, place a scallop in each warmed bowl and spoon a little velouté around. Place a lobster medallion next to a scallop and the ravioli on top. Dress with the micro basil.

'When we opened in Hammersmith, people were surprised, but we had a clear idea of what we wanted to do.'

ROSE GRAY & RUTH ROGERS
THE RIVER CAFÉ

Of all the restaurants that redefined British cooking in the 1980s, The River Café is the one that has had the longest and deepest impact. That hardly looked possible when it opened, despite early high ratings in *The Good Food Guide*. There was an Italian revolution going on – in Hammersmith? Readers reached for their *A–Z*s.

Rogers recalls that, when she and Gray opened, London W6 was 'much more the back of beyond than it is now'. Their intention was not only to unshackle fine dining from its old-school straitjacket, but also to bring a revitalised version of Italian food to the capital. Initially Tuscan-orientated, the menus slowly broadened as Gray and Rogers travelled the length and breadth of Italy, noting that Italian food varied not just from region to region or town to town, but even from family to family. The pair's commitment to freshness is such that the menus still change twice daily, depending on what's available. Even a dish as familiar as zuppa di vongole (see overleaf) can be reinterpreted in light of new experience, emphasising the dynamism that lies at the heart of all the best cooking.

Rose Gray
Ruth Rogers' cooking partner from the earliest inception of The River Café, Rose Gray, sadly died while this book was in production. It is relatively rare even now in the restaurant world for a successful business to be owned jointly and to be equally the product of two culinary intelligences, but that is how The River Café was run until 2010. Perhaps even more rarely in such a frenetic, competitive world, Rose Gray's passing was marked by a moment of universally fond, respectful tribute.

The River Café | Thames Wharf, Rainville Road, Hammersmith, London W6 9HA
(020) 7386 4200 | **www.rivercafe.co.uk**

Zuppa di vongole
Rose Gray & Ruth Rogers

SERVES 6

2kg small clams

2 tbsp extra virgin olive oil, plus extra for drizzling

3 garlic cloves, peeled and finely chopped

2 dried red chillies, crumbled

3 tbsp chopped flat-leaf parsley

750ml dry white wine, such as Vermentino

Slices of sourdough bread

1 Rinse the clams in cold water and then allow them to sit in fresh cold water for 10 minutes. Rinse again. Check over the clams and discard any that are not closed.

2 Heat the olive oil in a heavy-based saucepan that is large enough to hold the clams. Add the garlic and chillies and half the parsley and cook over a medium heat for 2–3 minutes. Add the wine, bring to the boil, cook for 1 minute and then add the clams. Stir well to coat the clams with the wine.

3 Cover the saucepan with a lid. Bring back to the boil, reduce the heat a little and cook the clams for 2–3 minutes or until they open. Discard any that remain closed.

4 Meanwhile, toast or grill the bread until brown, then prop up the pieces around the sides of 6 warmed dishes. With a slotted spoon, remove the clams to the dish. Reduce the wine in the saucepan for a few minutes more, then pour over the clams.

5 Sprinkle over the remaining parsley and drizzle with plenty of extra virgin olive oil.

'This is a recipe we were taught in Tuscany a few years ago. It uses the very strong bread-making traditions of the region and celebrates the fact that you're only an hour from the coast.'

JIMMY GRAHAM
OSTLERS CLOSE

In his own quiet way Jimmy Graham has always been something of a food crusader. An old hand at the restaurant game (Ostlers Close has been a stalwart of *The Good Food Guide* for 28 years), Graham was foraging for wild foods and growing his own insecticide-free soft fruit, herbs and vegetables long before it became fashionable.

This carefully nurtured domesticity is backed up by an established network of local and regional suppliers, and so successful is the formula that the small, modestly appointed restaurant that Jimmy Graham runs with his wife Amanda changes little from year to year. But there's no sign of coasting.

The Grahams remain as enthusiastic as ever, maintaining a balance between keeping customers happy with old favourites and evolving the style to avoid stagnation. Ideas are straightforward and well conceived. Jimmy loves to cook and eat game — but local seafood is also a strong suit.

'After picking wild mushrooms, growing my own produce is my next passion. I love to be able to pick my own vegetables and herbs knowing I'll be using them an hour later in the kitchen.'

Ostlers Close | 25 Bonnygate, Cupar, Fife KY15 4BU
(01334) 655574 | **www.ostlersclose.co.uk**

Fillet of hake with crispy Serrano ham and a stir-fry of sultanas and pine nuts with a sherry sauce
Jimmy Graham

SERVES 4

FOR THE SHERRY SAUCE

125ml fish stock

75ml white wine

50ml fino sherry

20ml milk or single cream

100g chilled unsalted butter, diced

Salt and freshly ground black pepper

FOR THE HAKE

4 fillets of hake, about 80g each

Olive oil, for cooking

2 slices of Serrano ham, cut in half

FOR THE STIR-FRY

30g butternut squash, peeled and finely diced

10g pine nuts

10g sultanas, soaked in 25ml fino sherry the night before, then drained

1 spring onion, trimmed and finely sliced

1 Preheat the oven to 200°C/Gas 6.

2 To make the sherry sauce, put the fish stock into a saucepan, bring to the boil and reduce by half (about 5 minutes), then add the wine and sherry and reduce by half again (another 5 minutes). Add the milk and stir in before adding the diced butter, either using a hand blender or liquidising the sauce to finish. Adjust the seasoning, adding salt and pepper if needed, and keep warm.

3 To cook the fish, heat 2 tbsp of olive oil in a lidded, non-stick frying pan over a medium heat. Season the fish fillets and add them to the pan. Cook for about 2 minutes or until the fish is opaque, then place the lid on top and remove to a warm place for 3–4 minutes or until the fish has finished steaming through.

4 Lay the ham on an oiled baking tray and put in the oven for 4–6 minutes or until crisp. Remove from the oven and leave to rest for 1 minute, before using.

5 Meanwhile, heat 1 tbsp of olive oil in a frying pan and stir-fry the butternut squash until softened. Add the pine nuts, sultanas and spring onion and stir until heated through. Season to taste.

6 To serve, place the hake, skin side up, on 4 warmed plates. Divide the stir-fry between the plates, top with the crispy ham and then spoon over the sauce.

'This dish reflects our love of Spain. I enjoy the simple combination of ingredients, the contrast of textures and flavours and the fact that different fish, such as seared scallops, can be substituted.'

SHANE OSBORN
PIED À TERRE

It still sometimes comes as a surprise to be reminded that great chefs are made, not born. Made, trained and drilled, that is. When he was 15, Shane Osborn took an apprenticeship in French cookery in Perth, Western Australia, where he grew up. Arriving in London in 1990, he cooked under Marcus Wareing at L'Oranger and Philip Howard at The Square, before arriving at Pied à Terre, on the end-to-end restaurant strip that is Charlotte Street.

Head chef since 2000, Osborn has elevated the place from a well-kept secret of those in the gastronomic know to one of *The Good Food Guide*'s Top 10 restaurants in the UK, with a style of food that hasn't been shy of innovative complexity, while still being founded on classical French principles. Through all the waves of gastronomic fashion, he has retained the chef's perpetual excitement at great ingredients, and he believes in retaining regular clients by allowing his menus free rein to keep evolving.

The fondness for elaboration is these days counter-balanced by a move towards simpler sauces and marinades. It makes for a lighter, healthier approach to grand dining. Shane Osborn has mixed feelings about some of the wilder experiments going on elsewhere: 'The forgotten word these days is "delicious". People want good food that they understand.'

Feet on the ground
In an era when fashionable eating in London moved in favour of massive gastrodomes, Pied à Terre defiantly represented the opposite end of the spectrum. Small, low-lit, well-appointed, it remains a picture of calm civility when full, a place where the time-hallowed twin purposes of eating out – relaxed conversation and stunning food – are allowed their due priority.

Pied à Terre | 34 Charlotte Street, Fitzrovia, London W1T 2NH
(020) 7636 1178 | **www.pied-a-terre.co.uk**

'Food has evolved so much in this city in the last 20 years. There's a real buzz when new places open, and the competition is so stiff it keeps you on your toes.'

Skate wing poached in beurre noisette with suckling pig belly

Shane Osborn

SERVES 4–6

FOR THE PORK BELLY
1 suckling pig belly or 1kg pork belly, skin on
100g sea salt
3 garlic cloves, peeled and sliced
Bunch of thyme
Duck fat

FOR THE SKATE WING
1kg skate wing
Salt and freshly ground black pepper

FOR THE BEURRE NOISETTE
100g unsalted butter
65ml brown chicken stock

FOR THE CHANTERELLE MUSHROOMS
25ml olive oil
1 garlic clove, peeled and chopped
50g chanterelle mushrooms
50ml white wine vinegar
50ml sweet wine

FOR THE ROSCOFF ONIONS
2–3 Roscoff onions, peeled and cut in half
30ml white balsamic vinegar
60ml lemon oil

TO GARNISH
Dried sweetcorn powder
Blanched sweetcorn kernels

Specific equipment: see page 259

1 For the pork belly, rub the belly with the sea salt, garlic and thyme and then place in the fridge overnight. The next day, preheat the oven to 180°C/Gas 4. Rinse off the salt mix and place the belly in a large saucepan of duck fat. Cook for 2½–3 hours or until tender and allow to drain on a rack. Transfer the pork onto a baking tray lined with greaseproof paper and press another tray on top. Put in the fridge for 2–3 hours or until firm.

2 Remove the flesh from both sides of the skate wing, remove any skin and lightly season. Cut into 80–90g pieces each about 7.5cm wide and roll each one into a sausage shape using cling film. Allow to set in the fridge for about 1 hour.

3 Just before you are ready to cook the skate rolls, make the beurre noisette. Place the butter in a hot saucepan and when the butter melts and separates, reduce the heat. As the milk solids at the bottom begin to brown (the beurre noisette), add the chicken stock. Remove from the heat and stir the butter until it reduces and curdles.

4 Place the skate rolls into a sous-vide bag (or two each into microwave fish bags), add the beurre noisette and seal as tightly as possible. Cook in a deep saucepan of water, making sure the seal of the bag is above the water line, for 12–15 minutes, adjusting the temperature to keep it at 58°C.

5 For the chanterelle mushrooms, heat the oil in a small pan and add the garlic followed by the chanterelles and a pinch of salt. Sauté until all the water from the mushrooms has evaporated. Add the vinegar and reduce until dry, then add the wine and reduce by two thirds.

6 To cook the onions, preheat the oven to 160°C/Gas 3. Rub the cut side of the onions with salt and the vinegar and lemon oil. Wrap them in foil and bake for about 30 minutes or until tender. Set aside in a warm place. Increase the temperature of the oven to 200°C/Gas 6.

7 Remove the bones from the pork and cut it into wedges. Place in a non-stick ovenproof pan, skin side down. Gently bring up to a hot temperature and then place in the oven for 2–3 minutes. Remove the skate from the bag and pat dry. Tip the beurre noisette into a saucepan to reheat. Take the belly from the oven and remove from the pan. Place the skate rolls in the pan to lightly brown all over and reheat in the residual heat from the pan.

8 To serve, brush some of the oil from the pork roasting pan onto each warmed plate. Sprinkle with corn powder, tapping off the excess, and then place two pieces of the belly onto each plate together with a skate roll. Cut the onion halves into smaller sections and add to the plates with the sweetcorn kernels and chanterelles and then pour over the beurre noisette. In the restaurant, we like to top the dish with puffed wild rice and a sweetcorn beignet.

'This is a very modern-looking dish, but soundly based on traditional principles. We should remember that classic dishes work for a reason.'

CHRIS BRADLEY
MR UNDERHILL'S

Ludlow owes its place on the foodie map in no small part to the efforts of Chris and Judy Bradley, who arrived in the late 1990s from their Suffolk restaurant of the same name. They seem to have been here forever, the setting of their restaurant-with-rooms oozing timeless charm (although those who choose to overnight here don't go without modern comforts). The little campus of converted outbuildings and gardens overlooking Dinham Weir is itself overlooked by the town's castle. Many readers of *The Good Food Guide* are drawn back by what the Guide calls 'a hands-on set-up *par excellence*'.

'Most of our dishes are built around three elements, which gives them the yumminess that people like.'

With Scotsman Chris in the kitchen, Judy runs front of house, tailoring her approach to the customer. If you want a hearty discussion about wines from a 'stunner' of a list, that's fine; if you prefer being left in peace, your wish will be respected. The menu, too, can be tweaked to embrace individual requirements but, in essence, the whole dining room eats from the same, daily-changing seven-courser, giving a sense of community to the proceedings as diners eye up dishes brought to customers who are a course ahead, or smile benignly as someone is given a plate of something that they've just proclaimed wonderful.

Mr Underhill's | Dinham Weir, Ludlow, Shropshire SY8 1EH
(01584) 874431 | **www.mr-underhills.co.uk**

Hake on a bed of warm tomatoes with chorizo crumbs
Chris Bradley

SERVES 4

4 fillets of hake, about 60g each
Salt and freshly ground black pepper
4 large plum tomatoes
Olive oil, to cover the tomatoes, plus 2 tbsp
100g breadcrumbs
25g butter, melted

FOR THE DRESSING

4 mini chorizos or slices of chorizo, finely diced
2 tbsp groundnut oil
English mustard powder
Runny honey
Lemon juice

1 Preheat the oven to 130°C/Gas ½. Lightly season the fish with salt, and put to one side. This will improve the flavour and help to create a dry surface for the breadcrumbs.

2 Bring a small saucepan of water to the boil and blanch the tomatoes in the water for 1–2 minutes. Transfer with a slotted spoon to a bowl of cold water and peel them. Cut into quarters lengthways and deseed, then lightly salt the tomatoes and leave for 15 minutes for the salt to soak in.

3 Place the tomatoes in a small, ovenproof dish, cover with olive oil and warm in the oven for 20–30 minutes.

4 For the dressing, gently fry the chorizo in the groundnut oil. Drain off the now chorizo-flavoured oil for the dressing and put the chorizo crumbs to one side to keep warm.

5 Make up the dressing in the following proportions: to every 10 parts chorizo oil, add a small pinch of mustard, 1 part honey and 2 parts lemon juice. Whisk the ingredients together to create a thick vinaigrette, adding salt and pepper to taste.

6 When you are ready to start cooking, preheat the oven to 180°C/Gas 4 and spread the breadcrumbs on a plate. Brush the skinless side of the hake with the melted butter and then press this side into the breadcrumbs – remember that you are only crumbing one side of the fish.

7 Heat the 2 tbsp of olive oil in a frying pan, add the fish, crumb side down, and fry for 3–4 minutes or until golden, then turn onto a baking tray crumb side up. Bake in the oven for about 5 minutes – the timing will vary depending on the oven and the thickness of the fish. To check it is ready, gently press the fish with your finger; it should feel firm rather than hard.

8 Trim the irregular edges of the tomatoes to make rectangles and lay onto warmed plates. Put the hake on top, surround with a dessert spoon of the dressing and sprinkle with chorizo crumbs.

'I always associate hake with Spain, so we introduced the Mediterranean influence. Use cured sweet chorizo, not the cooking stuff, which can give a fatty finish.'

BRUCE POOLE
CHEZ BRUCE

French city dwellers would immediately recognise the smart-looking place facing Wandsworth Common as a *restaurant du quartier*, somewhere the locals can eat with confidence when they don't fancy heading further afield. Since the 1980s, though, when Marco Pierre White opened here, 2 Bellevue Road, London SW17, has also attracted a much further-flung clientele.

Chez Bruce arose on this spot in 1995, when Bruce Poole went into business with White's former partners. 'We all liked the same food,' he says, and the focal point of the operation has never wavered. What is offered here is a style of French-based food that has almost become an endangered species in the UK (and perhaps even in France itself). There may be a modern sensibility to the dishes, but they never depart entirely from their roots in classic regional French cooking.

'We attempt to cook what most customers want to eat,' says Poole, and the intention finds its echo in the often-expressed view of diners that it's the kind of menu from which you could happily choose anything. If the breathless experimentation in modern British cooking has led to a globalisation of the national palate, one of the prices we have paid for that lies in some loss of appreciation of the food of our nearest neighbours. This is a loss that a springtime dish of braised peas and ham (see overleaf) sets about rectifying.

▌**Chez Bruce** | 2 Bellevue Road, Wandsworth, London SW17 7EG
▌(020) 8672 0114 | **www.chezbruce.co.uk**

'Developing classic dishes has always been more satisfying than "inventing" things simply for the sake of it. It's like great music – there's always so much more to discover.'

Peas braised with shaved fennel, butter and mint, served with pata negra ham

Bruce Poole

SERVES 4

½ small fennel bulb
250g frozen or fresh peas
75g unsalted butter
Salt and freshly ground black pepper
Mint leaves, chopped
Few drops of lemon juice
8 small slices of pata negra ham (or 4 slices of Parma ham), roughly chopped

1 Cut away the core of the fennel bulb and shave into wafer-thin slices on a mandoline or using a very sharp knife. If there are any fennel leaves, set aside.
2 If using fresh peas, boil in salted water until cooked and then refresh in iced water.
3 In a large saucepan on a medium-low heat, heat the frozen or blanched fresh peas with the butter and a small splash of water. When the peas have reached a pleasing buttery mass, add the fennel and stir in to warm through. Avoid overcooking or the fennel will quickly discolour.
4 Check the seasoning, adding salt and pepper if needed, and add plenty of mint (and fennel leaves if you have them) and a few drops of lemon juice.
5 Serve in warmed bowls with the ham scattered over and with a good grind of black pepper.

'I've always loved the combination of ham and peas. You could eat it as a starter, or it makes a lovely accompaniment for fish or lamb.'

'My grandparents were both Greek and preparing food was always a special occasion with them, so I started dabbling in cooking.'

ANTHONY DEMETRE
ARBUTUS

When Anthony Demetre and Will Smith teamed up to open Arbutus in 2006, they had no idea of the effect they would have on the London eating scene. Previously, Demetre had been cooking fairly demanding dishes with a high level of culinary ambition and lots of luxurious ingredients, but he sensed a shift in the market. Drawing on influences from early mentors, such as Gary Rhodes and his passion for British cooking, Demetre came up with a more unvarnished style of mostly European comfort food as his blueprint for Arbutus, based around slow cooking, cheaper cuts of meat and less fashionable types of fish. It's been so successful that he opened a second restaurant, Wild Honey, in Mayfair in 2007 and the formula is now being adopted by many other chefs. Not bad for someone who became a chef by accident: Demetre joined the navy in order to become a naval airman, but a knee problem meant he was 'ruthlessly discharged' – he just 'fell into food instead'.

Fine dining without tablecloths
As with his food, Anthony Demetre has hit upon a winning form of presentation. Arbutus, with its appealing, bistro-style setting and lively atmosphere, is located in the heart of Soho. Here diners can choose to sit along neat rows of closely ranked tables or perch at the bar, enjoying generous quantities of the crusty house bread while they pore over the menu.

Arbutus | 63–64 Frith Street, Soho, London W1D 3JW
(020) 7734 4545 | www.arbutusrestaurant.co.uk

Slow-cooked crisp pork belly with Herefordshire snails and carrot purée

Anthony Demetre

SERVES 6

FOR THE PORK IN BRINE
90g salt, plus extra for cooking the pork
90g caster sugar
Scant 2 tsp sel rose or preserving salt
1.5kg boneless pork belly, skin on

FOR ROASTING THE PORK
2 garlic bulbs
2 sprigs of thyme
Olive oil, for cooking

FOR THE GARLIC CONFIT
1 large garlic bulb
Salt and freshly ground black pepper
Duck fat, for cooking

FOR THE SNAIL BOUILLON
1 onion, peeled and diced
1 carrot, peeled and diced
1 celery stick, diced
24 de-shelled, precooked snails
Sprig of thyme
Sprig of rosemary
Handful of parsley stalks, leaves reserved
   and chopped
1 bay leaf
4 white peppercorns
Knob of butter

FOR THE CARROT PURÉE
400g carrots, peeled and finely chopped
100ml chicken stock
100g butter
1 bay leaf

TO SERVE
2 radishes, trimmed and thinly sliced
Micro salad leaves

1 To make the brine, bring 1 litre of water to the boil, add the salt, caster sugar and sel rose or preserving salt. Once the sugar and salts have dissolved, remove the pan from the heat and leave to cool. When cold, immerse the pork belly and leave it for 24 hours.
2 The next day, take the pork from the brine and place in a saucepan of cold water. Bring to the boil, then transfer the pork to a dish and leave to cool slightly. Preheat the oven to 160°C/Gas 3.
3 To roast the pork, place the garlic and thyme on the bottom of a roasting tin, put the pork on top, rind side up, and liberally drizzle with olive oil and sprinkle with salt. Pour 2cm of water into the tin, transfer to the oven and roast for 1½–2 hours, topping up with water now and again to stop it drying out.
4 When the pork is cooked through, remove it from the oven and leave to cool. Pour off all the juices and reserve. Place a tray or board on top of the pork and apply 3–4 plates to press and reshape the meat in order to obtain a nice, flat appearance (otherwise it develops an odd shape when cooling).
5 For the garlic confit, pick out the 12 largest, most perfect cloves in their skin from the garlic bulb, reserving the rest (peeled) for the snail bouillon. Cover the garlic cloves with cold water in a small saucepan and bring to the boil. Drain off the water and repeat the process another two times. Peel the garlic and cook in warm, seasoned duck fat in a separate saucepan on a low temperature for about 40 minutes or until tender.
6 For the snail bouillon, place the onion, carrot, celery, the reserved garlic and the snails in a saucepan with the herbs and peppercorns. Cover with cold water and bring to the boil. Then remove from the heat, season and set aside.
7 To make the carrot purée, put all the ingredients in a saucepan, bring to the boil, then reduce the heat and simmer for about 10 minutes or until the carrots are tender. Remove the bay leaf and blitz in a food processor or with a hand blender until smooth.
8 Slowly crisp the pork belly, skin side down, in a dry non-stick frying pan over a medium heat. Remove the snails and garlic cloves from the bouillon with a slotted spoon and transfer them to a clean pan. Add a little of the snail juice and the knob of butter. Bring to the boil, add the reserved chopped parsley leaves and correct the seasoning, if necessary. Warm the carrot purée in a pan, whisking to ensure it stays smooth.
9 When the pork belly is crisp, arrange it and the snails and garlic confit on 6 warmed plates and garnish with the radish slices and micro salad leaves.

'When creating a dish, I always look at what would be the natural diet for that particular animal. Pigs eat snails and the two together make really quite a beautiful dish.'

'I have changed to a "less is more" philosophy, and have been keeping the food simpler. I also consider the finer details of food sourcing more than ever before.'

TOM AIKENS
TOM AIKENS

Tom Aikens has been cooking professionally since the age of 16, when he got his first commis chef job at Mirabelle in Eastbourne, but his early exposure to food and wine came from his father and grandfather who were both wine merchants. 'From the age of 12, I spent a lot of my time on holiday in France, travelling with my father when he went to meet new suppliers or wholesalers. There were some days when I would end up working in the vineyards, sweeping out the cellars, sometimes having lunch.'

After Mirabelle, Aikens moved to London to work under David Cavalier at Cavalier's, then to The Capital Hotel with Philip Britten. Aged just 22, Aikens worked with Pierre Koffmann at La Tante Claire and, in 1993, he was appointed sous chef at Pied à Terre under Richard Neat. Then, after a year off gaining experience in France with Joël Robuchon and Gérard Boyer, he returned to London and re-joined Pied à Terre as head chef and co-proprietor. Aikens cites Koffmann and Robuchon as his greatest influences for different reasons, noting, 'Pierre taught me the skills of speed and organisation, while Joël taught me about attention to detail and routines of working.'

Aikens opened his eponymous Chelsea restaurant in 2003 and his meticulous modern French cooking continues to impress. Even more remarkable is the fact that he has achieved stardom and celebrity status without hawking himself around the celeb-chef TV circuit. He's happy to let his food do the talking.

Tom Aikens | 43 Elystan Street, Chelsea, London SW3 3NT
(020) 7584 2003 | **www.tomaikens.co.uk**

Foie gras and artichoke terrine
Tom Aikens

MAKES 12–15 SLICES

FOR THE FOIE GRAS
1 whole foie gras
200g sea salt

FOR THE ARTICHOKE PURÉE
300ml olive oil
10–12 banana shallots, peeled and chopped
6 garlic cloves, peeled and sliced
Large sprig of thyme
Salt and freshly ground black pepper
300ml white wine vinegar
400ml white wine
10–15 globe artichokes
100–150ml double cream
50ml truffle oil
Squeeze of lemon juice
2g gelatine leaves

FOR THE CELERIAC AND TRUFFLE REMOULADE
2 egg yolks
1 tbsp white wine vinegar
½ tsp French mustard
Juice of ½ lemon
200ml groundnut oil
100ml truffle oil
1 small celeriac, peeled and finely sliced
2 summer truffles, finely sliced

Specific equipment:
see page 259

1 Leave the foie gras at room temperature for 3 hours or until soft. Cover a baking sheet with cling film. Open up the foie gras and, with a sharp knife, cut through the liver until you find the veins. Carefully part the soft liver around the veins so that you can remove the whole vein network. Place the foie gras on the lined baking sheet and cover with another piece of cling film. Roll to an 8mm-thick rectangle measuring 28cm in length and 15cm in width and place in the freezer to set for about 45 minutes or until firm.

2 Sprinkle both sides of the foie gras with the sea salt and leave in the fridge for 6 hours. Brush off the salt, removing any remaining grains with a palette knife. Cut the foie gras into 4 equal 15cm-long rectangles and return to the fridge once again.

3 For the artichoke purée, put the olive oil into a large saucepan and add the shallots, garlic, thyme, 15g of salt and a good grinding of pepper. Cover with a lid and cook on a low heat for 3–4 minutes. Then add the vinegar and simmer to reduce by half. Add the white wine and reduce by half again, then add 2 litres of water. Bring to the boil, reduce the heat and simmer for 5 minutes. Check the seasoning.

4 Meanwhile, prepare the artichokes. Cut off the long stems and, with a sharp knife, trim off the main leaves of the flower, leaving just the choke and the layer of fine petals covering it. Add the artichokes to the water and cook for 15–20 minutes until just soft, or until you can place a knife in the centre of each and the choke drops off. Leave the artichokes to cool in the cooking liquor and then remove with a slotted spoon.

5 Remove the centre core of each artichoke and discard. Cut each remaining disc into a square, removing and saving the round edges, then place on a dry cloth. Place the trimmings into a saucepan with 100–150ml of the cooking liquor. Add the cream, truffle oil and a touch of lemon juice. Check the seasoning and then simmer the liquid for about 10 minutes or until reduced and sticky in consistency.

6 Meanwhile, soak the gelatine in cold water for about 5 minutes to soften and then squeeze to drain. Put the artichoke sauce into a blender and add the gelatine. Purée, pass this through a fine sieve and leave to cool for 10 minutes.

7 Line a 15 x 8 x 8cm terrine mould with a double layer of cling film, ensuring there is enough coming over the edges of the mould to cover the top of the terrine. Then place a single piece of foie gras in the bottom. Add a little of the artichoke purée and then a layer of artichoke hearts. Add some more purée and then the next layer of foie gras. Carry on the process until it is all layered up, finishing with foie gras. Then wrap very tightly in cling film and put in the fridge to chill for 4–5 hours.

8 To make the remoulade, first make the mayonnaise. Mix the yolks, vinegar, mustard and lemon juice in a bowl, add ½ tsp of salt and some pepper and whisk well until emulsified. Then slowly add the groundnut oil. If it gets too thick, add a little water. Add the truffle oil and check the seasoning.

9 To finish, mix the mayonnaise with the celeriac and add half the truffles. Put a layer of the remoulade and some of the remaining truffle slices onto each serving plate. Unwrap the terrine and cut into slices, place on top of the remoulade and serve immediately.

'I have always loved this recipe for its simplicity and beauty. The richness of the foie gras goes well with the acidity of the artichoke.'

'I want to create great restaurants for people to enjoy terrific regional foods, well cooked and served with style and in a professional manner.'

MICHAEL CAINES
GIDLEIGH PARK

Michael Caines first came to the attention of *The Good Food Guide* in the mid 1990s when he took over from Shaun Hill as head chef at handsome Gidleigh Park in Devon. A local lad who had already worked for Raymond Blanc, Joël Robuchon and Bernard Loiseau, Caines made quite an impression on the inspector, who predicted in the 1995 Guide that, 'he will very soon be established as one of the country's top chefs'.

Caines has created an innovative style of his own, using his classical French training to get the best out of regional produce, and he has become a champion of the West Country's rich larder – as demonstrated by dishes such as Brixham scallops with black truffles, caramelised cauliflower purée and sweet raisin vinaigrette. After 15 years at the top of his game, Caines says he has gradually evolved as a chef rather than abruptly changing: 'My cooking style has developed, as has my presentation, but the goals remain the same – to work wherever possible with local and seasonal produce and cook it to the highest standard in an imaginative way.'

Working through a crisis
Two months into his job at Gidleigh, Caines suffered a terrible car accident in which he lost his right arm, but such was his determination to succeed that he was back in the kitchen full time after only four weeks. Some 15 years later and with an MBE to his name, Caines is still at the helm at Gidleigh Park but also oversees the other restaurants in the fast-expanding ABode group of hotels.

Gidleigh Park | Chagford, Devon TQ13 8HH
(01647) 432367 | **www.gidleigh.com**

Pan-fried duck foie gras and braised chicory with orange and raisins
Michael Caines

SERVES 4

FOR THE RAISINS SOAKED IN JASMINE TEA (MAKE 3 DAYS AHEAD)
200ml boiling water
5g jasmine tea leaves
100g raisins

FOR THE BRAISED CHICORY
50g onions, peeled and finely chopped
1 garlic clove, peeled and chopped
25g butter
Salt and freshly ground black pepper
200ml orange juice
50ml chicken stock
Sprig of thyme
1 small bay leaf
4 baby chicory bulbs

FOR THE ORANGE SAUCE
Pinch of orange powder made from ground dried orange zest, plus extra for dusting
Squeeze of orange juice

FOR THE CARAMELISED WALNUTS
100g caster sugar
75g shelled walnut halves

FOR THE FOIE GRAS
4 pieces of duck foie gras, about 80g each
Sea salt

TO SERVE
Flat-leaf parsley
Micro salad leaves

1 For the raisins, pour the boiling water over the tea leaves in a bowl and leave until the water has cooled a little for the flavour to infuse. Place the raisins in a jar or plastic container and then pour the tea through a fine sieve onto the raisins. Leave them to soak for 3 days before using to allow the raisins to plump up.

2 To braise the chicory, preheat the oven to 180°C/Gas 4. In an ovenproof frying pan, sweat the onions and garlic in the butter with a pinch of salt for about 5 minutes without browning. Add the orange juice, chicken stock, thyme and bay leaf and stir. Then add the baby chicory bulbs and seasoning and bring to the boil. Cover with a piece of baking parchment and then a lid and braise in the oven for 20–25 minutes or until soft. Leave to cool.

3 Remove the braised chicory and strain the stock through a sieve. Transfer most of the stock to a small saucepan, and place the chicory in the remaining stock and set aside.

4 To make the orange sauce, bring the stock in the saucepan to the boil, add a pinch of the orange powder and season with salt and pepper. Then add a drop of orange juice and set aside for serving.

5 For the caramelised walnuts, dissolve the sugar in 100ml of water in a saucepan over a low heat and then bring to the boil. Add the walnuts and boil until the water turns to a syrup and reaches 110°C. Heat a deep-fat fryer to 190°C, then remove the nuts with a slotted spoon from the syrup and place in the fryer for 1–2 minutes or until golden brown. Remove the caramelised walnuts, place them on baking parchment and salt lightly. Once cool, take a few of the nuts, reserving the rest, and chop for the topping of the foie gras.

6 In a hot, non-stick frying pan, fry the foie gras for about 30 seconds on each side or until browned. Remove from the pan and top with the chopped walnuts, a dusting of orange powder and some sea salt. Leave to rest in a warm place.

7 To serve, reheat the chicory in its stock and warm the raisins in their juices. Cut each chicory bulb in half and put two halves in the middle of each warmed plate. Sprinkle the raisins around and place the foie gras on top. Add a few caramelised walnuts, spoon over some of the orange sauce and garnish with the flat-leaf parsley and micro salad leaves.

'Putting together the chicory and citrus orange fruit with the pan-fried foie gras, is a glorious venture of taste.'

JONRAY & PETER SANCHEZ-IGLESIAS

CASAMIA

First, there were the Roux brothers and more recently the Galvins, but the latest chef siblings to make a mark on the British restaurant scene are Jonray (to the right in the photograph above) and Peter Sanchez-Iglesias of Casamia. These brothers were only 23 and 21 when they took over their parents' Italian restaurant in a leafy suburb of Bristol and swapped pizzas and tiramisu for wild wood pigeon with coffee and almonds, followed by strawberry soup and balsamic caramel ice cream.

Citing Ferran Adrià, Heston Blumenthal and 'our Spanish dad' as their foodie influences, they have created a style of their own, ripping up the rule book with daring, modern variations on Italian classics. Using the best produce they can get their hands on, they have embraced cutting-edge techniques for dishes as innovative as roast breast of chicken served with a confit of its wings, amaretto flavours and carrots in different textures. Named as Best Up-and-Coming Chefs in *The Good Food Guide 2008*, they were described as 'genuinely exciting newcomers' thanks to their original, beautifully presented cooking, underpinned by genuine passion and ambition.

'We are always planning several years ahead so we know what direction we are going in. That really keeps things fresh.'

Casamia | 38 High Street, Westbury on Trym, Bristol BS9 3DZ
(0117) 959 2884 | **www.casamiarestaurant.co.uk**

ASAMIA

atureja montana
Winter Savory
ry, excellent for salt free diets
used to treat colic & fungal infections

Traditional beetroot risotto with pickled fennel, pistachios and iced yogurt
Jonray & Peter Sanchez-Iglesias

SERVES 4–6

FOR THE ICED YOGURT
100ml whole milk
50ml stock syrup
60g liquid glucose
500g natural yogurt

FOR THE BEETROOT STOCK
8 beetroot
2 sprigs of thyme
25ml olive oil
1 banana shallot, peeled and chopped
1 garlic clove, peeled and chopped
1 bay leaf
15ml white wine vinegar

FOR THE BEETROOT CREAM
15ml olive oil
1 banana shallot, peeled and chopped
1 garlic clove, peeled and chopped
1 bay leaf
Small handful of thyme
100ml double cream
75ml whole milk

FOR THE RISOTTO
50ml olive oil
2 shallots, peeled and chopped
200g aged carnaroli rice
50ml medium-dry white wine
½ garlic clove, peeled and lightly crushed

200g Parmesan cheese, grated
Salt and freshly ground black pepper

FOR THE PICKLED FENNEL
1 fennel bulb, shaved finely on a mandoline or with a sharp knife
200ml white wine vinegar
100ml still mineral water

TO SERVE
Chopped pistachios
Finely snipped chives

Specific equipment: see page 259

1 For the iced yogurt, place the milk, syrup and glucose in a saucepan, bring to a simmer and whisk together. Leave to cool, then add the yogurt and blend with a hand-held electric mixer to a smooth consistency. Once blended, pass the mixture through a fine sieve into a freezable container and leave in the fridge for 8 hours. Transfer to the freezer to set for 24 hours.

2 To make the beetroot stock, preheat the oven to 200°C/Gas 6. Peel the beetroot. Place the peelings on a baking tray with the thyme and cook in the oven for 15 minutes or until the peelings are roasted. Juice the beetroot in a blender to make a pulp.

3 Heat the olive oil in a large, heavy-based saucepan and sweat the shallot and garlic over a low heat for about 5 minutes without browning. Then add the roasted peelings, half the beetroot pulp and the bay leaf. Fry for 3 minutes and add the white wine vinegar to deglaze. Just cover the ingredients with water, heat to 60°C and then remove the saucepan from the heat. Allow the stock to infuse for 6–8 hours and then pass through a fine sieve. Store in the fridge until ready to use.

4 To make the beetroot cream, repeat step 3 using the ingredients listed together with half of the remaining beetroot pulp and, instead of adding water, use the cream and milk. Heat to 60°C and then remove the saucepan from the heat. Allow the cream to infuse for 6–8 hours and then pass through a fine sieve. Place in a bowl or fill up a cream whipper and refrigerate overnight. Leave the remaining beetroot pulp in the fridge overnight, too.

5 To make the risotto, heat the beetroot stock in a saucepan. In a separate, large pan heat the olive oil and cook the shallots on a medium heat for about 6 minutes to soften. Add the rice and lightly toast it. Then add the white wine, bring to the boil, reduce the heat and simmer until the liquid has almost completely evaporated.

6 Add the garlic and 250ml of the beetroot stock and simmer it to reduce by half, while stirring. Add another 250ml of the stock and, once again, allow it to reduce by half. Keep adding and reducing the beetroot stock until the rice is al dente and creamy (you won't use all of the stock). Spread the risotto evenly across a cold baking tray and leave in a cool place to cool. Then transfer to the fridge.

7 When it is time to serve, pickle the fennel. Put the shavings in a jar and cover with the wine vinegar and water. The fennel will absorb the vinegar instantly and remain crunchy.

8 Gently heat the risotto with 100ml of the remaining beetroot stock. Bring to the boil and then add enough of the beetroot cream until you have a loose creamy consistency, stirring continuously. Take the pan off the heat and add the Parmesan cheese, to taste, stirring rapidly. If the risotto is too heavy, add some more beetroot cream to lighten. Add seasoning to taste.

9 Put the risotto into 4–6 warmed bowls and top with slices of the pickled fennel and some pistachios and chives. Add quenelles of the iced yogurt and serve immediately. In the restaurant, we like to top the dish with our puffed saffron rice.

'My cooking style has definitely become simpler over the years. The emphasis is less on what dishes look like than achieving great flavours.'

ROBERT THOMPSON
ROBERT THOMPSON AT THE HAMBROUGH

While it is true that the culinary arts can be learned at any age, there nonetheless remains no substitute for starting early. Robert Thompson knew he wanted to be a chef from the age of ten, and chalked up his first *stage* as a washer-upper when he was 13 years old. From those modest but assiduous beginnings, via some very illustrious addresses (such as Winteringham Fields and Cliveden), he arrived in the summer of 2008 on the Isle of Wight.

It's fair to say the island hasn't been among the pace-setting regions for ambitious cookery in the past, but all that has now changed. What's more, there is a bountiful natural larder growing in its own microclimate. The island's famous garlic, celebrated in an annual festival, is joined by wonderful asparagus and a multitude of potato varieties that Thompson happily admits to not previously having heard of. The seafood is another obvious lure. Crab, lobster and sea bass are all of unparalleled quality, as is the turbot that forms the centrepiece of Thompson's dazzling main course (see overleaf).

Dining room with a view
If location is all, the Hambrough has a head start. It stands on the southeast edge of the Isle of Wight in a street of elegant Victorian townhouses overlooking Ventnor's esplanade. Diners enjoy soul-soothing views towards the harbour and out over the wide blue Channel, before their attention is firmly diverted by the finest cooking on the island.

Robert Thompson at the Hambrough | Hambrough Road, Ventnor, Isle of Wight PO38 1SQ
(01983) 856333 | **www.thehambrough.com**

Pan-roasted fillet of turbot with gratin of razor clam and tomato and watercress

Robert Thompson

SERVES 4

FOR THE WATERCRESS PURÉE

2 bunches of watercress

50ml double cream

Salt and freshly ground black pepper

FOR THE RISOTTO

600ml chicken stock

2 shallots, peeled and finely chopped, reserving the trimmings

Olive oil, for cooking

200g risotto rice

100ml white wine

20g crème fraîche

10g black truffle, finely chopped (or 2 tbsp truffle oil)

20g Parmesan cheese, finely grated

FOR THE CLAMS AND TOMATOES

4 razor clams

Splash of white wine

200g tomatoes of varied colours and size, sliced

20g white breadcrumbs

2 tsp finely grated Parmesan cheese

Extra virgin olive oil

Squeeze of lemon juice

FOR THE TURBOT

4 turbot fillet steaks, about 175g each

Knob of unsalted butter

Squeeze of lemon juice

Pinch of fleur de sel (optional)

1 For the watercress purée, remove 12 nice small watercress leaves for garnishing the dish and also approximately 15 large leaves for the gratin of razor clam. Plunge the rest of the watercress into boiling water and instantly refresh in iced water. Squeeze as much water out of the watercress as possible.

2 Bring the double cream to the boil in a small saucepan and then add the watercress. Transfer to a blender and liquidise to a smooth green purée. Season with salt and pepper.

3 For the risotto, bring the chicken stock to the boil in a saucepan. In another saucepan gently sweat the shallots in a little olive oil over a medium heat for about 5 minutes or until soft. Add the rice and cook for a further 2 minutes or until the grains are well coated in the oil. Add the wine and continue to cook over a fairly moderate heat for about 3 minutes or until reduced and the mix hisses drily again. Little by little, add the boiling chicken stock to the pan while stirring. Continue to cook for 12–15 minutes or until the rice is cooked but still has a bite.

4 For the clams, sweat the reserved shallot trimmings in a little olive oil, add the clams and wine and quickly cover the pan with a lid. Cook for about 2 minutes or until the clams have opened enough to remove the meat. Allow to cool slightly.

5 Pick out the clam meat. Throw out the darker tube and coarsely chop the rest. Cut any small tomatoes in half and larger ones into 5mm dice. Finely slice the 15 reserved watercress leaves. Then carefully clean the razor shells, ensuring each half remains attached down the centre, and place on a baking tray. Add a line of watercress purée down the centre of each shell and top with the chopped clams, some of the pieces of tomato and all the chopped watercress. Finish with a scattering of breadcrumbs, the Parmesan cheese and seasoning.

6 For the tomato mixture, put the remaining tomatoes in a bowl together with some olive oil and a little lemon juice. Stir well and season according to taste.

7 To finish the risotto, gently reheat, adding the crème fraîche, truffle (or truffle oil) and Parmesan cheese. Season well.

8 Preheat the oven to 190°C/Gas 5. Season the turbot lightly and place in a hot non-stick, ovenproof pan with a little olive oil and brown on one side before transferring the pan to the oven. Cook for 2–3 minutes or until the fish gives slightly when pressed and remove from the oven. Cook the dressed razor clam shells in the oven for 2 minutes. Preheat the grill to hot.

9 Meanwhile, add the butter to the turbot pan and baste the fish for 20 seconds before adding the lemon juice to finish. Remove from the pan and re-season with a small amount of fleur de sel, if using, or add some more salt.

10 Finish the clams under the grill for about 2 minutes or until just browned.

11 To serve, drag a line of watercress purée across each warmed plate. Place some risotto at one end and top with the turbot. Lay a razor clam across each plate and then place the tomato mixture around. Garnish with the reserved watercress leaves. In the restaurant, we like to top the dish with 2 truffle slices.

'People are far more aware these days of what they're eating. They want to taste what's written on the menu.'

'I liked the buzz of the kitchen when I was a kid. Dad was a chef. At eight years old, I was turning toast over for him on the breakfast shift.'

NATHAN OUTLAW
RESTAURANT NATHAN OUTLAW

Nathan Outlaw is down to earth, very likeable and has a pure philosophy on food that ensures only the best raw produce is used in his kitchen. He set a formidable pace at his previous venue in Fowey and was awarded *The Good Food Guide*'s Restaurant Newcomer of the Year in 2008. But the opportunity to relocate his restaurant to the St Enodoc Hotel in Rock has upped the stakes considerably.

Seafood, local produce, natural flavours and the avoidance of gimmicks have always been watchwords, but the move gave Outlaw the chance to explore modern fish cookery in greater depth – 80 per cent of the menu now comprises Cornish-landed fish. The traditional staples of most seafood restaurants – bouillabaisse, fruits de mer and the like – are not part of the repertoire here; the ideas are entirely Outlaw's own.

Confident from the start, when it came to training, Outlaw wanted nothing but the best. Working under Peter Kromberg at the much-acclaimed Le Soufflé in the InterContinental Hotel is where it all began. There were then two years with Rick Stein at The Seafood Restaurant, where he fell in love with Cornwall, and then with John Campbell at Lords of the Manor and The Vineyard at Stockcross. Outlaw is now considered one of the UK's foremost chefs. Indeed, the 2011 Guide awarded him the Editors' Best Fish Restaurant.

Restaurant Nathan Outlaw | St Enodoc Hotel, Rock Road, Rock, Cornwall PL27 6LA
(01208) 863394 | **www.nathan-outlaw.com**

Cornish salt ling, squid and mussel stew

Nathan Outlaw

SERVES 4

FOR THE LING

1.5–2kg ling, cut into 4 x 200g pieces
Sea salt
Olive oil, for cooking and serving
Small handful of tarragon, chopped
Small handful of chervil, chopped

FOR THE SHELLFISH STOCK

1kg frozen prawns in their shells
Olive oil, for cooking
1 onion, peeled and chopped
2 carrots, peeled and chopped
4 tomatoes, chopped
6 garlic cloves, peeled and halved
Grated zest and juice of 1 orange

FOR THE MUSSELS

500g live mussels, scrubbed and beards
    removed

FOR THE SAFFRON SAUCE

2 tomatoes, chopped
Sprig of tarragon
Pinch of saffron
50g unsalted butter

FOR THE VEGETABLES

100g peeled and roughly chopped potato
1 leek, trimmed and cut into short lengths

FOR THE SQUID

Olive oil, for cooking
2 squid, prepared and cut into rings
Salt and freshly ground black pepper

1 Cover the ling with sea salt, leave for 1 hour in the fridge and then wash off the salt and dry the fish.

2 To make the shellfish stock, preheat the oven to 180°C/Gas 4. Place the prawns on a baking tray and roast for 45 minutes. Heat some olive oil in a saucepan and sweat the onion, carrots, tomatoes, garlic and orange zest for about 4 minutes or until lightly browned, and then add the prawns. Cover with water and the orange juice and leave to simmer for 1 hour. Pass the stock through a sieve into a fresh pan (discard the rest of the ingredients) and reduce by three quarters. Leave to cool and then chill.

3 To cook the mussels, heat a pan with a tight-fitting lid to hot and then add the mussels. Add 100ml of water, cover the pan and bring to the boil. Steam the mussels for 1 minute to open them then drain, retaining the liquid.

4 Pick out the mussels from the shells and chill. Strain the liquid through muslin and also chill. When cold, wash the mussels in the liquid and then strain the mussel stock again into a clean container. Repeat several times until no grit remains. Discard the liquid and chill the mussels.

5 To make the saffron sauce, put the tomatoes, tarragon and saffron into a pan along with 200ml of the shellfish stock. Bring to the boil and then reduce by three quarters. Blend in a food processor, pass through a sieve and keep warm.

6 To prepare the vegetables, cook the potato in a pan of lightly salted water for about 20 minutes or until soft. Drain and, when cool, cut into 1cm dice. Blanch the leek in boiling water for 1 minute, drain and refresh in cold water.

7 For the ling, preheat the oven to 200°C/Gas 6. Heat some olive oil in a non-stick frying pan and, when hot, add the fish, presentation side down. Cook on a medium heat for 2–3 minutes or until slightly golden and then transfer to a baking tray and cook in the oven for 3 minutes. Flip the fish over and cook for 1 minute, then, right at the end, add most of the tarragon and chervil, reserving some for garnishing.

8 Meanwhile, cook the squid. Heat a non-stick pan on a medium heat. Add some olive oil and, when it is hot, add the squid. Sauté for about 1 minute or until cooked and season with salt and pepper.

9 Bring the saffron sauce to the boil, add the butter and seasoning, if necessary. Then add the vegetables and mussels, heat for 2 minutes and taste for seasoning. Divide the sauce, vegetables and mussels between 4 large warmed soup plates, place the ling and squid on top and serve immediately, scattering over the remaining tarragon and chervil and adding some olive oil.

'Ling is plentiful and cheap but flaky to handle. Salting for an hour draws out the moisture and gives the fish a meaty texture.'

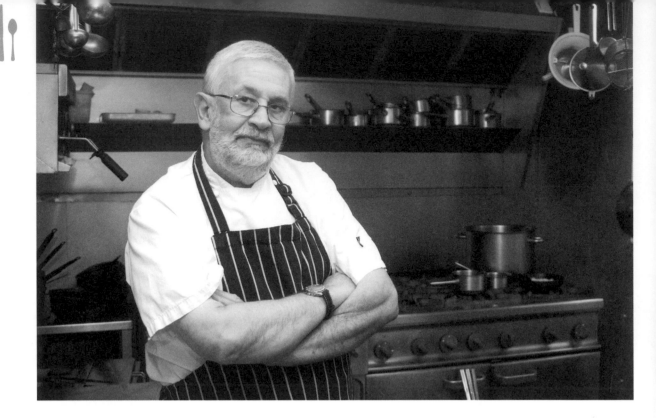

STEPHEN MARKWICK
CULINARIA

At the age of 63, Stephen Markwick still cooks every dish at his Bristol bistro Culinaria. 'Feeding people has always been in my nature and I still get a great buzz cooking for a full restaurant,' says Markwick, who started cooking in the 1960s at The Savoy when the ovens were still fired by coal. His biggest influence has been George Perry-Smith, who ran The Hole in the Wall in Bath. In 1973, Markwick spotted an advertisement in *The Times* for a chef to work for Perry-Smith and this led to a job at the latter's new restaurant, The Carved Angel, in Dartmouth with Joyce Molyneux. This was then followed by a spell working alongside Perry-Smith at The Riverside in Helford.

> *'I have always been a traditional chef in my thinking – new fads don't work for me.'*

In 1980, Markwick and his wife Judy opened their first restaurant, Bistro 21, in Bristol, which was crowned Bistro of the Year in *The Good Food Guide 1983*. 'George Perry-Smith-style food at knock-down prices' is how the Guide described Markwick's menu – Provençal fish soup, tarragon chicken, crab tart and St Emilion au chocolat. These dishes still appear on the menu at Culinaria. Markwick says, 'You have to bring passion to your cooking and not over-complicate dishes. Flavour should be the first priority – and, of course, sticking to the seasons.'

Culinaria | 1 Chandos Road, Bristol BS6 6PG
(0117) 973 7999 | **www.culinariabristol.co.uk**

Squid with red wine, orange and fennel
Stephen Markwick

SERVES 4

500g squid, prepared and cleaned

2 fresh or tinned tomatoes (optional)

1 onion, peeled and thinly sliced

1 leek, trimmed and thinly sliced

½ fennel bulb, trimmed and thinly sliced

4 garlic cloves, peeled and thinly sliced

3 tbsp olive oil

1 dessertspoon fennel seeds (or 1 tsp ground fennel)

1 dessertspoon dill seeds (or 1 tsp ground dill)

1 dessertspoon coriander seeds (or 1 tsp ground coriander)

2 small hot bird's eye chillies, deseeded and sliced

1 tbsp tomato paste

Grated zest and juice of 2 oranges

375ml full-bodied red wine

Salt and freshly ground black pepper

Small handful of coriander, chopped

FOR THE ORANGE GREMOLATA

2 garlic cloves, peeled and finely chopped

Small handful of flat-leaf or curly parsley, finely chopped

Grated zest of 1 orange

1 Preheat the oven to 150°C/Gas 2. Wash the squid to make sure there's no grit left in it. Cut the body into rings, the wings into strips and leave the tentacles in longish pieces. Leave in a colander to drain.

2 If you are using fresh tomatoes, skin them by bringing a saucepan of water to the boil and blanching the tomatoes in the water for 1–2 minutes. Transfer them to a bowl of cold water with a slotted spoon and then peel and chop. If you are using tinned tomatoes, just cut them into pieces.

3 Fry the onion, leek, fennel and garlic in a casserole dish with the olive oil on a medium heat for about 5 minutes or until starting to soften. Grind the fennel, dill and coriander seeds (if using seeds) using a pestle and mortar or coffee grinder and add the ground spices to the vegetables along with the chillies. Fry on a high heat for 2 minutes then add the squid. (You need to make sure the vegetables and spices are hot before you fry the squid or it will stew rather than fry.)

4 Cook the ingredients together briefly, then add the tomato paste, chopped tomatoes (if using), orange zest and juice and red wine. Season well with salt and pepper. Bring to simmering point, then cover with a lid and cook in the oven for 1–1½ hours or until tender (the cooking time will depend on the size of the squid).

5 To make the gremolata, mix all the ingredients together.

6 To serve, adjust the seasoning of the squid, if necessary, and add the coriander. Serve with either rice or croutons and a sprinkling of the orange gremolata.

'The combination of the orange and chilli works well with the red wine, and the slow braising brings it together. It is the intensity of the flavours that does it for me.'

TESSA BRAMLEY
THE OLD VICARAGE

Ten minutes from Sheffield, but rooted firmly in the country, The Old Vicarage is a long-standing favourite of *The Good Food Guide*, having been named Newcomer of the Year in 1988. Tessa Bramley's leadership and nature-led philosophy is absolutely key to the success of the restaurant. The mid 19th-century country house, with its lovely mature grounds, looks like Hollywood's idea of an English rural hideaway, but the food and the welcome (often from Bramley herself), are anything but stuffy, staid or dusty.

Fittingly, for a self-taught chef (with a little help from her grandmother) who claims to have fallen into the trade by accident, Bramley's style is intuitive, sometimes daring. Her knowledge of unusual and wild ingredients is put to use in dishes such as sweet woodruff ice cream or strawberry and sweet cicely soufflé. Stuffed with goodies from the kitchen garden and beyond, the menu offers genuinely interesting flavour combinations, rather dashingly presented, in this most traditional of settings.

Vicarage Wine Cellars
The Old Vicarage is also the base for Vicarage Wine Cellars, and restaurant customers reap the rewards of its carefully nurtured relationships with highly regarded and progressive producers from both the New and Old World; the wine list is as thoughtfully constructed as the menu. With Bramley around, that means very thoughtfully indeed.

The Old Vicarage | Ridgeway Moor, Ridgeway, Derbyshire S12 3XW
(0114) 247 5814 | **www.theoldvicarage.co.uk**

'The farm I look at through the window grows lovely new potatoes and our game and guinea fowl are from across the valley.'

Sea bass with mango and crab salsa, potato galette and mint and pea sabayon
Tessa Bramley

SERVES 4

FOR THE LEMON OIL
8 tbsp extra virgin olive oil
Grated zest and juice of 1 lemon
1 fat garlic clove, peeled and bruised
Pinch of salt
Pinch of sugar

FOR THE CRAB SALSA
100g crab claw meat
100g peeled and finely diced mango
4 spring onions, trimmed and chopped
5cm piece of cucumber, peeled, deseeded
  and finely diced
Salt and freshly ground black pepper

FOR THE GALETTES
150g unsalted butter
500g waxy new potatoes, such as Charlotte
  or Jersey Royal, peeled and thinly sliced
Handful of chervil, chopped

FOR THE SEA BASS
4 fillets of wild sea bass
Olive oil, for preparing the fish
Unsalted butter
2 leeks, trimmed and cut into pieces

FOR THE PEA AND MINT SABAYON
6 shallots, peeled and finely chopped
2 garlic cloves, peeled and finely chopped
2 tbsp olive oil
Bunch of mint, tied together
250ml Muscat dessert wine
600ml fish stock, plus 4 tbsp, heated
300ml double cream
6 tbsp frozen peas
1 egg yolk

TO SERVE
Asparagus tips, spinach and peas

1 To make the lemon oil, mix the olive oil with the rest of the ingredients and leave (for several days, if possible) to infuse.
2 To make the crab salsa, toss the ingredients together in a bowl, adding 1 tbsp of the infused lemon oil. Season to taste and put in the fridge to chill for a few hours.
3 For the galettes, gently melt the butter in a saucepan until the butter separates. Skim off the top layer of froth with a spoon and remove the pan from the heat. Leave the remaining butter to cool for a few minutes and then strain through a fine sieve to make clarified butter.
4 Dip the potatoes in the clarified butter and arrange half the slices in an overlapping layer in a frying pan. Season lightly, add the chervil and then top with a second layer of potatoes. Pour over the rest of the butter. Gently cook the galette on a low heat for about 2 minutes or until golden, then turn over and cook the other side for a further 2 minutes or until golden and cooked through.
5 Slash the skin of each sea bass fillet with a sharp knife and rub the fillets all over with oil. Set aside.
6 To begin the sabayon, gently sweat the shallots and garlic in the oil over a medium heat for about 5 minutes without browning. Add the mint and wine, bring to the boil and let the sauce reduce by half, which will take 5–10 minutes. Then add the stock and reduce the sauce again by half, which will take another 5–10 minutes. Add the cream and reduce by half once more (another 5–10 minutes). Season to taste, add the peas and bring back to the boil.
7 Remove the mint and immediately blend the sauce to ensure it remains green. Pass through a chinois or fine sieve into a clean pan and check the seasoning one more time.
8 In a metal bowl over a pan of simmering water, whisk the egg yolk with the 4 tbsp of hot fish stock, whisking vigorously for 5–10 minutes or until thick and dense. To finish the sabayon, fold spoonfuls of the egg mixture into the sauce until it is light and fluffy. Keep warm.
9 Preheat the oven to 240°C/Gas 9 and heat a dry, non-stick frying pan to hot. Sear the fish, skin side down for 2–3 minutes or until golden. Reduce the heat and add a knob of the butter. Put the leek pieces on the base of a roasting tin. Set the fish on top, skin side up and roast in the oven for about 3 minutes or until just cooked – the trivet of leeks keeps the fish pearly white and moist.
10 Cook the asparagus tips, spinach and peas until tender and drain. Cut the galette into 4 neatly trimmed portions. Assemble the dish on 4 warmed plates with a galette topped with the leeks and asparagus. Add the sea bass with some crab salsa, spoon the sabayon around and add the peas.

'I don't want food to be boring or just something you put in your mouth because you're hungry, I want it to be an experience.'

WILL HOLLAND
LA BÉCASSE

Will Holland only ever wanted to be a chef. At the age of 14, when most of his school friends were doing paper rounds to earn their pocket money, Holland had a Saturday job at his local butcher. He says it was always in him to be a chef and it was eating well as a family that gave him an understanding of good food. His main influence was watching fellow Bristolian Keith Floyd's cookery shows on TV, and he admits that he once wrote to *Jim'll Fix It*, asking if he could cook with Floyd.

After college and working in local restaurants in Bristol, Holland worked at Homewood Park Hotel in Bath and Gravetye Manor in Sussex. But it was with Alan Murchison at L'Ortolan in 2004 that his true star potential was spotted. When Murchison bought the Hibiscus restaurant in Ludlow and reopened it as La Bécasse in July 2007, he appointed Holland as head chef and gave him free rein over the menus.

Within the restaurant's ancient stone and wood-panelled walls, Holland's modern British interpretation of classic cuisine gained him many accolades before he had even turned thirty. Holland explains that he strives for 'exciting presentation and unusual flavour combinations but not in a gimmicky way – simply because I believe they work.'

La Bécasse | 17 Corve Street, Ludlow, Shropshire SY8 1DA
(01584) 872325 | **www.labecasse.co.uk**

Halibut with cauliflower, Morteau sausage, honeycomb, lime and curry
Will Holland

SERVES 4

FOR THE CAULIFLOWER
1 small cauliflower
Salt and freshly ground black pepper
250ml milk
80g unsalted butter

FOR THE TEMPURA BATTER
½ tsp each coriander & cumin seeds
50g plain flour
35g cornflour
10g baking powder
1 tsp mixed garam masala, Madras curry powder, turmeric and black onion seeds
125ml chilled sparkling water

FOR THE CURRIED LIME EMULSION
½ tsp each coriander & cumin seeds
60ml light olive oil
20g roughly chopped onion
2 garlic cloves, peeled and chopped
1½ tsp mixed garam masala, Madras curry powder and turmeric
6 black peppercorns
1 cardamom pod
Grated zest and juice of 4 limes
25g caster sugar

FOR THE HONEYCOMB
110g caster sugar
15g clear honey
40g glucose
1 tsp bicarbonate of soda

FOR THE SAUCE AND LETTUCE
130g whole Morteau sausage
1 onion, celery stick, carrot and leek, each peeled and roughly chopped
3 garlic cloves, peeled and chopped
Sprig of thyme
1 bay leaf
6 black peppercorns
1 Little Gem lettuce
30ml light olive oil
50g unsalted butter

FOR THE HALIBUT
10ml light olive oil
4 halibut fillets, about 100g each
35g unsalted butter
45ml lime juice

1 Remove the leaves from the cauliflower and set aside. Cut the cauliflower in half and cut one half into 12 thin slices and 12 small florets. Blanch the florets for 2 minutes in boiling salted water, refresh in iced water and drain on kitchen paper. Set aside until required.

2 Chop the remaining cauliflower and leaves. Place in a saucepan with the milk and 250ml of water. Bring to the boil and simmer for 15–20 minutes or until soft. Drain and transfer to a blender with the butter and blitz to a purée. Season with salt. Pass through a fine sieve and set aside.

3 For the tempura batter, dry roast the coriander and cumin seeds in a frying pan over a high heat for 1–2 minutes or until aromatic. Allow to cool before transferring to a bowl. Add all the other ingredients except for the sparkling water. Mix well and set aside.

4 To make the curried lime emulsion, dry roast the coriander and cumin seeds in a pan over a high heat for 1–2 minutes or until aromatic. Reduce the heat to low and add the oil. Then add the onion and garlic and fry for 2 minutes before adding the remaining ingredients, except the lime and sugar. Sweat for 20 minutes, then pass the oil through muslin into a bowl. Combine 25ml of the curry oil with the lime zest and leave to infuse. Put the lime juice and sugar in a small pan, gently heat until the sugar has dissolved and then reduce until 50ml of syrup remains. Blitz with a hand blender and slowly add the curry oil until it is emulsified. Store in the fridge.

5 For the honeycomb, line a loaf tin with greaseproof paper. Place the sugar, honey and glucose in a saucepan with 20ml of water and place over a medium heat. Swirl the pan as the mixture starts to boil to mix, but don't stir. Heat to 155°C, then remove from the heat and sift the bicarbonate of soda over the surface. Stir gently to mix and tip into the lined tin. Allow the honeycomb to cool and set – do not move the tin or the air will be knocked from the honeycomb. Break into roughly equal-sized small pieces and store in an airtight container.

6 To cook the Morteau sausage, place the sausage, vegetables, garlic, herbs and peppercorns in a saucepan and cover with cold water. Bring to the boil, reduce the heat and simmer gently for 10 minutes. Remove from the heat and allow to cool before removing the Morteau sausage and setting aside to cool further. Pass the cooking liquor through a fine sieve and reserve. Cut the sausage into 5mm dice and refrigerate.

7 Cut the lettuce into four, lengthways. Heat a frying pan over a medium heat, add the oil and then the lettuce. Fry all sides until lightly golden, then add the butter and 200ml of the sausage stock and cook over a high heat for 6–8 minutes or until the lettuce is wilted and the stock and butter have reduced. Add the diced sausage to the pan to warm through.

8 To cook the halibut, heat a frying pan over a medium heat and add the oil. Lightly season the fillets with salt and fry over a medium-high heat for 3–4 minutes or until the fillets are cooked halfway through. Turn them over, add the butter and lime juice and remove from the heat. Allow to rest in the butter and lime juice, occasionally basting.

9 Place the reserved cauliflower slices on a piece of greaseproof paper and put in a steamer for 3 minutes. Remove and lightly season. Warm the cauliflower purée from step 2 in a small saucepan. Heat a deep-fat fryer to 175°C. Add the sparkling water to the tempura mix and whisk until smooth. Then add the blanched cauliflower florets. Strain any excess batter from the florets and deep-fry for 2 minutes or until golden and crispy. Remove from the fryer and drain on kitchen paper. Season with salt.

10 To serve, place a piece of wilted lettuce in the middle of each warmed bowl and top with a fillet of halibut. Put 3 spots of curried lime emulsion around the fish and add a deep-fried cauliflower floret on top of each spot. Then add 3 cauliflower slices and place a spoonful of cauliflower purée in the bowl. Finish with some Morteau sausage dice and honeycomb pieces.

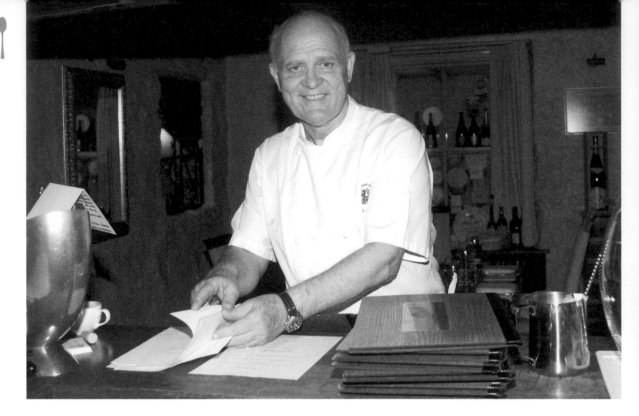

PETER JUKES
THE CELLAR

As a young chef at Chewton Glen and then at Gleneagles, Peter Jukes had no idea that lobsters cast their shells and that there was a season for fish. It was only when he came to work close to the source of the supply – buying fish directly off the Pittenweem boats for his own restaurant in Anstruther – that he finally learned about their seasonality. That was nearly 30 years ago.

The very best seasonal fish (now mostly from Peterhead and Aberdeen, with diver-caught scallops and mussels from the west coast) is still served as fresh as possible without masking the flavour with heavy sauces. Crayfish bisque is a longstanding favourite, and grilled halibut served with a pot of hollandaise is just as likely to be on the menu. Jukes cooks it just so and no more. Ideas have been fine-tuned over the years, and some dishes are hardy perennials, but the philosophy of keeping things simple, fresh and seasonal has established this hugely atmospheric former cooperage and herring smokery as one of the best seafood restaurants in Britain, ensuring a presence in *The Good Food Guide* for 27 years.

'For someone who comes from Wolverhampton and was brought up on fish fingers, it's strange that I've ended up in a Scottish fishing village cooking fish.'

The Cellar | 24 East Green, Anstruther, Fife KY10 3AA
(01333) 310378 | **www.cellaranstruther.co.uk**

THE
CELLAR

SPECIALISING
IN SEAFOOD
& FINE WINES

Baked fillet of wild halibut with pine nuts and bacon
Peter Jukes

SERVES 4

½ small Savoy cabbage, cut into strips

½ sweetheart cabbage, cut into strips

270g butter

500g Maris Piper potatoes, peeled and chopped

Salt and freshly ground black pepper

Splash of olive oil

Pinch of freshly grated nutmeg

4 smoked bacon rashers, chopped

50g pine nuts

4 halibut fillets, about 175g each and 1cm thick

Juice of 1 lemon

Sea salt

1 tbsp breadcrumbs

1 Preheat the oven to 200°C/Gas 6. Blanch all the cabbage strips in boiling water for 30 seconds. Refresh under cold water and then squeeze to drain.

2 Clarify 220g of the butter by gently melting it in a saucepan until the butter separates. Skim off the top layer of froth with a spoon and remove the pan from the heat. Leave the remaining butter to cool for a few minutes and then strain through a fine sieve to make clarified butter.

3 Meanwhile, put the potatoes in a large saucepan, cover with water, add a little salt and bring to the boil. Reduce the heat and leave to simmer for 15–20 minutes or until just cooked. Drain off the water and dry the potatoes by putting them in the oven for 2 minutes. Return to the pan and mash, beating in the remaining 50g of butter and the olive oil. Add nutmeg, to taste, and keep warm.

4 Cook the bacon in a separate large saucepan in the clarified butter. Add the pine nuts and brown slightly and then add the cabbage. Season and keep warm.

5 Season the halibut fillets with lemon juice and sea salt. Place on a baking tray and put the breadcrumbs on top of the fillets. Bake in the oven for 5–7 minutes or until cooked through.

6 To serve, place the cabbage mix on 4 warmed plates together with the mash. Put the halibut on top and pour around the juices from the baking tray. Accompany with steamed mange tout, green beans and broccoli.

'After 25 years I couldn't possibly take it off the menu – it's the benchmark Cellar dish, cooked to order and served straight from the oven to the plate.'

VINEET BHATIA
RASOI

'My food can't be pigeon-holed – it comes from all over India, but it is based on my passion to cook; it comes from my mind and from my heart.'

If you thought Indian cooking was all about onion bhajis and chicken tikka masala, think again. Vineet Bhatia has done more for the profile of Indian food in Britain than most, taking a fresh and inventive look at his native cuisine and inspiring Indian chefs in the UK to raise their game.

Back in his native Mumbai, however, the passion was for flying – Bhatia wanted to be a pilot, and always says he became a chef by mistake after being turned down by the Indian Air Force.

When he came to England in the mid 1990s to work at the Star of India in South Kensington, Bhatia found Indian cooking here 'pretty appalling' and was determined to change its image. A move to Zaika in 2001 allowed a consolidation of his style – a sophisticated, updated version of Indian food, the appeal of which lay in combining Eastern and Western ideas into novel, subtly spiced dishes; the delicate fish moilee (see overleaf) dates from this period.

By the time Bhatia and his wife Rashima opened their own restaurant in a Victorian Chelsea townhouse, turning it into the intimate and exotic Rasoi seven years ago, he had established himself as one of the foremost Indian chefs in the UK.

Rasoi | 10 Lincoln Street, Chelsea, London SW3 2TS
(020) 7225 1881 | **www.rasoi-uk.com**

Coastal fish moilee with cashew-tempered rice

Vineet Bhatia

SERVES 4

600g halibut fillet, cut into 50g chunks

2 tsp turmeric powder

4 tbsp lime juice

Salt

3–4 tbsp corn oil

1 tbsp mustard seeds

3 garlic cloves, peeled and chopped

Thumb-sized piece of fresh root ginger, peeled and cut into matchsticks

2 sprigs of curry leaves

80g peeled and sliced onions

2 green chillies, cut into half and deseeded

2 red chillies, cut into half and deseeded

1 tomato, sliced

600ml thick coconut milk

1 tsp crushed black peppercorns

FOR THE CASHEW-TEMPERED RICE

250g basmati rice

40g cashew nuts

2 tbsp corn oil

½ tbsp peeled and chopped fresh root ginger

80g peeled and chopped red onion

1 small green chilli, deseeded and chopped

1 tbsp chopped coriander leaves

1 Marinate the fish chunks in 1 tsp of the turmeric powder and 2 tbsp of the lime juice and a pinch of salt. Cover and set aside.

2 Heat the oil in a large heavy-based saucepan and add the mustard seeds. Once they begin to splutter, add the garlic, ginger, curry leaves and onions. Fry over a medium heat for about 5 minutes or until the onions become soft and then add all the chillies.

3 Add the remaining turmeric powder and sauté for about 1 minute and then add the tomato along with 100ml of water. Cook for another 5 minutes.

4 Add the coconut milk and bring to the boil. Strain the sauce into a new saucepan and then immediately transfer the marinated fish to the pan. Reduce the heat and gently poach for 3–5 minutes or until the halibut is cooked through. Adjust the seasonings with salt, the crushed pepper and remaining lime juice.

5 Meanwhile, make the cashew-tempered rice. Steam the rice for 12–15 minutes or until cooked. Toast the cashew nuts in a medium oven for 10 minutes and then roughly chop. Heat the oil in a non-stick wok, add the cashew nuts, ginger, onion and chilli and cook over a high heat until slightly browned. Toss the cooked rice into the wok and season lightly with salt.

6 When the rice is heated through, remove from the heat and transfer onto 4 warmed plates. Add the coconut fish and garnish the rice with the chopped coriander leaves. In the restaurant, we like to top the dish with some caviar, curry leaves and a red chilli.

'Inspired by the fishermen of Kerala, this is a simple, light, easy-to-make dish that's very creamy and moreish to eat.'

'It's easy to feel unconnected and remote up here, but I reckon 90 per cent of our business is from elsewhere in the UK, Europe and America.'

ALAN CRAIGIE
THE CREEL

When Alan and Joyce Craigie bought their property in the tiny hamlet of St Margaret's Hope in 1985, it represented a distinct change of scenery. Alan Craigie had previously been chef to the British consul-general in Los Angeles, but the journey from LA to Orkney has been a productive one and the investment of time and care has won The Creel a following that stretches all the way back to the American west coast.

The international reputation helps when you have chosen to pitch camp in such a far-flung outpost. All chefs talk of seasonality, but the concept has different implications at the northern fringes of the British Isles – it's well into the summer before local fruit and vegetables are ready. The compensation, of course, is some of the most fabulous seafood in the country. And fish has its seasons, too, as Craigie's son, now grown, attested when he said that the smell of herring cooking has always evoked summer for him.

As the decades have passed, Alan Craigie's cooking has developed in line with outside influences. He is as capable of being inspired by eating sardines from a street stall in Spain as he is on a family outing to Le Gavroche. His fried herring with cabbage (see overleaf) healthily reinterprets the Scots favourite, deep-fried herring in oatmeal, for a dish that he dubs 'the greatest fast food in the world'.

The Creel | Front Road, St Margaret's Hope, Highlands KW17 2SL
(01856) 831311 | **www.thecreel.co.uk**

Pan-fried herring fillets and roes with toasted oatmeal, Savoy cabbage and oven-dried tomatoes

Alan Craigie

SERVES 4

100g coarse oatmeal
Salt and freshly ground black pepper
4 tomatoes, cut in half
600g new potatoes, peeled
100g butter
115ml olive oil, plus a splash to serve
500g Savoy cabbage, thinly sliced
100g leeks, trimmed and sliced
100g shallots, peeled and sliced
3 garlic cloves, peeled and chopped
4 herring roes
Juice of ½ lemon, plus extra to serve
Bunch of parsley, chopped
Bunch of chives, chopped
8 large herring fillets

1 Preheat the oven to 100°C/Gas ¼. Toast the oatmeal in a dry, heavy-based, non-stick frying pan for 2 minutes on a medium heat. Stir constantly so the grains toast evenly.

2 Season the tomatoes, place on a baking tray, cut side up, and bake in the oven for 1½ hours.

3 Meanwhile, put the potatoes in a large saucepan, cover with water, add some salt and bring to the boil. Reduce the heat and leave to simmer for 10–15 minutes or until cooked. Drain and allow the potatoes to cool.

4 Gently melt half the butter and 30ml of the olive oil in a heavy-based pan. Add the cabbage, leeks, shallots and garlic, cover with a lid and let them sweat slowly for 5–10 minutes or until soft and tender, giving the mixture a good stir a few times during cooking. Season to taste.

5 Cut the potatoes into thick slices and pan-fry in 15ml of the olive oil until golden.

6 In a non-stick pan with the remaining olive oil and butter, fry the herring roes over a medium heat for 3–4 minutes, then add the lemon juice and the chopped parsley and most of the chives.

7 At the same time, cook the herring fillets in a clean, dry, non-stick frying pan for 3–4 minutes or until cooked through. When cooked, sprinkle each fillet with most of the toasted oatmeal.

8 To serve, sprinkle the remaining toasted oatmeal around 4 warmed plates. Spoon the Savoy cabbage mixture onto the middle of the plates and place the herring fillets on top of the cabbage. Add a little splash of olive oil and lemon juice and then arrange the herring roes, fried potatoes and roasted tomatoes around the fish. Garnish with the reserved chopped chives.

'Herring is one of the great fish of the world. It's so versatile, so good for you, and there's plenty of it.'

'The quality of produce is higher and far more varied now. With more private growers we can be even more precise with our seasonality.'

SALLY CLARKE
CLARKE'S

A champion of top-quality, seasonal produce long before it became fashionable, Sally Clarke can claim to be part of the British renaissance in cooking in the late 1980s. She launched Clarke's in 1984, fresh from four years in California, with cooking based on the emergent Californian cuisine of 'vibrant colours and flavours on the plate, lots of chargrilling, salsas/relishes, big, bold but pretty salads and short cooking times for vegetables.'

Clarke's no-choice, four-course dinners were groundbreaking, reflecting a simple approach with a fresh delicacy of flavour. It is only in the past few years that diners have been given a choice, but the idea of taking fresh seasonal produce and cooking it simply remains a winning formula. As if to prove this, Clarke's has been listed in *The Good Food Guide* for 27 years.

It is all served in two rooms — a basement restaurant with open-plan kitchen and a smaller ground-floor room — in a converted Victorian house. Next door is & Clarke's, a small café and shop selling bread, pastries, cheeses and a range of take-away dishes. Alice Waters, of the legendary Chez Panisse in Berkeley, California, is a friend and mentor, and Chez Panisse remains Clarke's favourite restaurant, her 'guiding light'.

Clarke's | 124 Kensington Church Street, Notting Hill, London W8 4BH
(020) 7221 9225 | **www.sallyclarke.com**

Roasted free-range chicken with soft Parmesan polenta and chestnuts

Sally Clarke

SERVES 4

1 x 1.5–2kg free-range chicken

1 large onion, peeled and cut into large chunks

1 large carrot, peeled and cut into large chunks

2 celery sticks, peeled and cut into large chunks

1 garlic bulb, roughly chopped, skin and all

3 tbsp mixed chopped rosemary, thyme and/or sage

Juice of 1 lemon

Olive oil

Sea salt and freshly ground black pepper

FOR THE PARMESAN POLENTA

500ml milk

2 bay leaves or sprigs of rosemary or thyme

1 garlic clove, peeled and crushed

200g polenta

20g butter

50g Parmesan cheese, grated

FOR THE CHESTNUTS

Small knob of butter

100g whole chestnuts, each roughly broken into 2–3 pieces

FOR THE SAUCE

2 tsp plain flour

2 glasses of full-bodied red wine

500ml chicken stock

TO SERVE

Watercress or bitter leaf salad

Steamed kale

1 Preheat the oven to 180°C/Gas 4. Trim the chicken of excess fat, neck skin and parson's nose, then place it in a roomy roasting tin with the vegetables, garlic, 2 tbsp of the chopped herbs, the lemon juice and a good drizzle of olive oil. Mix the ingredients together by hand, until all are well coated in the oil, massaging the herbs onto the skin of the chicken.

2 Push the vegetables into the centre of the tin and place the chicken, breast side up, on top. Season well. Place in the centre of the oven and roast for 10–20 minutes or until the skin has started to brown. Remove the pan from the oven and turn the chicken over, backbone side up. Turn down the heat to 160°C/Gas 3.

3 Continue to roast for another 20 minutes, then turn over and cook for a further 45 minutes, basting a couple of times with the garlicky-herby oil. Check it is cooked through by inserting a metal skewer into the thigh. If the juices run clear, the chicken is ready.

4 Meanwhile, make the polenta. Warm the milk with 500ml of water and the herbs, garlic and some seasoning for about 10 minutes. Do not let it simmer or boil. Strain the liquid into a clean pan and stir in the polenta over a low, simmering heat. Continue to cook for 10–15 minutes as it thickens. Cover and set aside.

5 For the chestnuts, melt the butter over a high heat, add the chestnut pieces and remaining 1 tbsp of chopped herbs and fry for about 5 minutes or until crisp. Season and leave in a warm place.

6 Remove the chicken from the oven and place it, breast side down, in a bowl, cover with a plate or cloth and allow to rest for up to 10 minutes in a warm (not hot) place.

7 Meanwhile, make the sauce. Drain the excess oil from the roasting tin, retain the vegetables but remove any burnt pieces. Place the tin on the stove and heat until it sizzles, sprinkle with the flour and stir well. Pour in the red wine and scrape the debris from the bottom of the tin into the juices. Add the stock and simmer, stirring as it thickens. Taste for seasoning, strain into a clean pan, skim any excess oil from the top, and keep warm.

8 Just before serving, stir the butter and three quarters of the Parmesan cheese into the polenta and season to taste. Carve the chicken into even-sized pieces. Place a spoonful of polenta and a chicken piece on 4 warmed plates. Scatter over the chestnuts and add the watercress salad and kale. At the table, sprinkle the remaining Parmesan over the polenta and serve with the sauce.

'This roast chicken has a very rustic feel and look – in the very early days we chargrilled many of our main courses.'

'I try to have original thoughts in the way I cook, recreating classics or using ingredients I know work together, if in an unexpected way.'

TRISTAN MASON
RESTAURANT TRISTAN

If there is one chef who is frequently overlooked it is Tristan Mason, yet he is, without doubt, one of Britain's rising stars. Restaurant Tristan is his first venture as chef-patron, an atmospheric, heavily beamed venue on the first floor of an ancient, timbered building in the old part of Horsham. It is here that this highly ambitious chef – who started off as a graphic design student pot washing in a professional kitchen to earn money and ended up working for Marco Pierre White and Paul Merrett ('he taught me to think outside the box') – has truly come of age.

Mason keeps his head down and focuses on the raw materials that pass through his kitchen. He trusts his judgement, lets ingredients speak for themselves and allows modern ideas to impinge freely on classic French techniques. Dishes are constantly evolving – he describes his roast duck with parsnip and vanilla purée (see overleaf) as one of those recipes 'where you have the ingredients and flavours bubbling away in your head', and each time it's been on the menu, 'it's been a little better.'

Restaurant Tristan | 3 Stans Way, East Street, Horsham, West Sussex RH12 1HU
(01403) 255688 | **www.restauranttristan.co.uk**

Roast duck with parsnip and vanilla purée, poached pear and spiced bread

Tristan Mason

SERVES 4

FOR THE SPICED BREAD
Small loaf of spiced bread or gingerbread

FOR THE PARSNIP AND VANILLA PURÉE
2 parsnips, peeled and finely chopped
200ml milk
65ml double cream
½ vanilla pod, split in half lengthways
40g butter
Salt and freshly ground black pepper

FOR THE POACHED PEARS
150g caster sugar
150g butter
4 conference pears, peeled, leaving the stalks on

FOR THE ROAST DUCK
4 Gressingham or Barbary duck breasts

TO SERVE
Micro herbs, or other herbs
Pea shoots

1 Preheat the oven to 100°C/Gas ¼ and line a baking tray with greaseproof paper. Slice the spiced bread as thinly as possible and make the rest into crumbs. Place the slices and crumbs on the baking tray and leave to dry in the oven for about 1 hour or until crisp. Remove from the oven and increase the temperature to 220°C/Gas 7.

2 Meanwhile, make the parsnip and vanilla purée. Put the parsnips into a saucepan, cover with the milk and cream and add the vanilla pod. Bring to the boil, then reduce the heat and simmer gently for about 20 minutes or until the parsnip is very tender. Take out the vanilla pod and blend the parsnip and cream mixture with the butter until silky smooth. Season to taste.

3 For the poached pears, put the sugar and butter in a saucepan, add 150ml of water and bring to the boil. Reduce the heat, carefully add the pears and let them simmer gently for about 30 minutes or until soft. Leave in the cooking liquor to cool slightly.

4 For the roast duck, heat a frying pan to a medium heat, season the duck breasts and place in the pan, skin side down. Cook for about 5 minutes or until the skin is golden, then quickly seal the other side. Transfer to a roasting tin, skin side down, and roast in the oven for about 8 minutes. Remove the duck breasts from the oven and allow to rest for 5 minutes.

5 To serve, stand a poached pear on each warmed plate and gently warm the parsnip purée. Spoon some purée down one side and sprinkle across a fine line of breadcrumbs. Slice a duck breast, arrange next to the pear and add the spiced bread, herbs and pea shoots.

'Adding the vanilla to the parsnip brings the whole dish together.'

'When I mentioned the importance of regional food to a well-known critic 20 years ago, I was laughed at, but now everybody's talking about it.'

RICHARD CORRIGAN
CORRIGAN'S MAYFAIR

Farmer's son Richard Corrigan wanted to be a chef from the moment he watched his mother bake bread in the kitchen of the family's thatched cottage in County Meath in rural Ireland. The house had just four rooms plus a dairy and larder outside, but the kitchen was the place where Corrigan got his first taste of good food, recalling, 'We had no money but we ate like kings — there was always home-salted belly pork, rabbits in the pot and homemade butter.' At the age of 14, he got a job at the local hotel and spent the summer 'peeling, washing, chopping, and slicing my fingers'. He was hooked.

At 21, Corrigan moved to London to work at Le Méridien Piccadilly and then at Mulligans, Bentley's and as head chef at Stephen Bull's Fulham Road restaurant, which is where *The Good Food Guide* first spotted him in 1994. Richard Corrigan opened his first restaurant, Lindsay House, in 1997 and it remained one of London's most acclaimed restaurants for more than a decade.

Corrigan's earthy, yet sophisticated, cooking is now showcased at Corrigan's Mayfair. Robust dishes, such as roe deer Wellington with pickled cabbage, remain true to his Irish roots and he is a loyal supporter of artisan producers. 'I grew up on a farm, so I like to see my money going straight back to the producers instead of the middlemen.'

Corrigan's Mayfair | 28 Upper Grosvenor Street, Mayfair, London W1K 7EH
(020) 7499 9943 | **www.corrigansmayfair.com**

Game bird salad with romesco sauce
Richard Corrigan

SERVES 4

2 partridges
2 mallards
Salt and freshly ground black pepper
Small handful of thyme
2 garlic cloves, peeled and chopped
Olive oil, for frying
Duck fat, for roasting

FOR THE ROMESCO SAUCE

50g almonds
2 small red peppers
5 tomatoes
20ml sherry vinegar
20g caster sugar
1 tbsp olive oil
1 onion, peeled and finely diced
1 fat garlic clove, peeled and grated
½ small red chilli, deseeded and very
   finely chopped

TO SERVE

Green salad
Parma ham

1 Preheat the oven to 180°C/Gas 4. To prepare the game birds, remove and discard the legs (or ask your butcher to do this for you) and lightly season the remaining carcases with salt, pepper, thyme and garlic. Cover and leave them to stand for at least 2 hours. Then seal in a hot, non-stick frying pan in some olive oil before transferring to a roasting tin and roasting in duck fat for 40–60 minutes or until the meat is soft and tender, but still pink, and the skin crispy.

2 When the birds are cooked, remove from the oven (but keep it turned on) and leave to rest for 10 minutes.

3 Meanwhile, make the sauce. Toast the almonds in the oven for 10 minutes, then remove, allow to cool, chop and set aside. At the same time, roast the peppers in a roasting tin in the oven for about 20 minutes or until charred. Place in a large bowl, cover with cling film and leave to cool. Then remove the skin and deseed and cut into 1 cm dice.

4 Take the eyes out of the tomatoes and cut a cross in the bottom of each, then blanch in lightly salted hot water for 5 seconds before transferring into iced water. Drain the water, then skin the tomatoes, cut in half and remove the seeds. Cut into pieces the same size as the pepper.

5 Put the sherry vinegar and sugar into a small saucepan, bring to the boil, lower the heat and simmer to reduce to a syrup. Remove from the heat.

6 In a separate pan, heat the olive oil and sweat the onion, garlic and chilli over a medium heat for about 5 minutes or until soft. Add the tomatoes and cook for about 10 minutes or until reduced by half. Then add the red peppers and remove from the heat.

7 When cooled slightly, add the vinegar and sugar syrup and the toasted almonds.

8 To serve, remove the wishbones from the carcases by cutting around the bone on either side and pulling and twisting with your fingers. Cut the breasts from the carcases and carve into slices lengthways.

9 Pile the romesco sauce onto 4 serving plates, add slices of the game birds and top with a green salad and slices of Parma ham.

'I'm a farmer's son so I feel a real connection with producers, with tradition and with seasonality.'

FRANCES ATKINS
THE YORKE ARMS

Since opening The Yorke Arms in 1997, Frances Atkins has established herself as one of the leading female chefs in the country. Over the years, *The Good Food Guide* has tracked her from a Buckinghamshire pub, via a country house hotel in Scotland and a Chelsea restaurant to this hugely atmospheric creeper-clad coaching inn overlooking Ramsgill's tiny village green. Furthermore, The Yorke Arms was rated as Readers' Restaurant of the Year in the 2008 Guide.

'Becoming a chef was in my blood, something I always wanted to do since a child.'

It represents a return to home territory for Atkins – she hails from nearby Ilkley and learned her trade at that stalwart of early editions of *The Good Food Guide*, The Box Tree – and she leads a kitchen that is proudly aware of its roots. Culinary influences are as diverse as Elizabeth David, Raymond Blanc and the Roux brothers and her style has developed into a blend of classic thinking with assured technique and an instinctive feel for ingredients. Atkins' cooking, although based on simple ideas and well-tried combinations, contrives to introduce new twists and original touches, such as teaming chocolate with pigeon in the recipe overleaf.

The Yorke Arms | Ramsgill, Yorkshire HG3 5RL
(01423) 755243 | **www.yorke-arms.co.uk**

Oven-roasted squab pigeon with oxtail and a chocolate sauce
Frances Atkins

SERVES 4

FOR THE OXTAIL

Olive oil, for cooking

1 oxtail, weighing about 500g, cut into pieces

1 leek, trimmed and chopped

1 onion, peeled and chopped

1 carrot, peeled and chopped

2 garlic cloves, peeled and chopped

300ml red wine

600ml chicken stock

Salt and freshly ground black pepper

Bunch of mixed herbs

FOR THE PIGEONS

2 oven-ready squab pigeons

Melted duck fat or olive oil

1 leek, trimmed and chopped

1 carrot, peeled and chopped

2 tbsp sherry vinegar

100ml port

4 pancetta rashers

Salt and white pepper

2 bunches of thyme

Handful of dark chocolate buttons (70% cocoa solids)

FOR THE CARAMELISED SHALLOTS

8–10 shallots, peeled and kept whole

Red wine

2 tbsp caster sugar

Large knob of butter

FOR THE CROUTES

4 slices of white bread

Olive oil, for frying

TO SERVE

Buttered cabbage, potato purée, sautéed wild mushrooms, steamed baby carrots

1 Preheat the oven to 160°C/Gas 3. Heat some olive oil in a large casserole dish and sauté the oxtail, vegetables and garlic for 5–10 minutes or until browned. Deglaze the casserole with the red wine and stock and then add seasoning and the mixed herbs.

2 Cook in the oven for about 3 hours or until the oxtail is tender. The liquid should have reduced by half (if the liquid is reducing too quickly, add a little water during cooking) and the meat should be falling away from the bone.

3 Take out of the oven and leave to cool. Remove the oxtail from the bone, finely chop it and place in a bowl with just enough of the juices to cover the meat. Strain the rest of the juices, place in a container and leave in the fridge together with the oxtail until the next day. Then remove the layer of fat from the meat and juices.

4 To prepare the pigeons, remove the legs and half of each wing joint. Place the legs in a saucepan and cover with duck fat or oil and simmer for 30–45 minutes, depending on their size, until soft.

5 Preheat the oven to 200°C/Gas 6. Heat some olive oil in a separate saucepan and then sauté the wing joints with the leek and carrot over a high heat for about 10 minutes or until browned. Deglaze the pan with the sherry vinegar and port, bring to the boil and then reduce by half. Strain and set aside.

6 Place a pancetta rasher lengthways across each breast and season. Inside each carcase place a bunch of thyme and half wrap the birds in foil, leaving the bacon exposed. Transfer to a roasting tin and roast for 15–20 minutes or until cooked through. Remove from the oven, turn upside down and leave to rest for 10 minutes. Remove the bacon and cut the breasts from each carcase.

7 To caramelise the shallots, put them into a saucepan, cover with a little red wine and cook on a medium heat for 10–15 minutes or until soft. Add the sugar and butter and cook for 3–5 minutes or until the sugar has dissolved and the mix has a rich sweet/sour flavour.

8 To make the croutes, trim the slices of white bread into rounds and fry in olive oil until crisp.

9 Add the juices from the oxtail to the pigeon sauce from step 5, bring to the boil and reduce to 150ml. Correct the seasoning, if necessary, and add the chocolate buttons. This should give the right balance of chocolate in the sauce so it will not become overly sweet and yet produce a good glaze.

10 To serve, warm the oxtail meat in a small pan over a low heat. Then, on each plate, arrange some oxtail with the pigeon breast and the legs on a croute together with some caramelised shallots. Serve with the cabbage, potato purée, wild mushrooms and baby carrots.

'The addition of chocolate is designed to stimulate the taste buds so you feel the need to eat a little more.'

MICHEL ROUX JR
LE GAVROCHE

As culinary institutions go, Le Gavroche is one of the more venerable.
It has been serving French haute cuisine to a chic Mayfair clientele since
1967, and took up permanent residence in *The Good Food Guide* soon
after opening. Stars from many different firmaments have passed through
the famous basement room, signed the guest book and been captured in
framed photographs on the elegant green walls.

  Le Gavroche was the first British venture of the convivial Roux brothers,
Albert and Michel, part of that generation that began to elevate fine dining
in the UK to another level. Albert's son, Michel Jr, took up the reins in 1991,
having virtually, as he puts it, 'been brought up amid the sounds and smells
of the kitchen'. It was a culinary education that gave him the confidence to
maintain Le Gavroche's formidable reputation for consistency, while gently seeing the
menus into the modern era. Although the place has maintained its commitment to
formality, there is nonetheless a happy buzz at most sessions, with big tables replicating
the festive ambience of eating out *en famille* in France. Menus are written in both
languages and Michel's cooking also seeks to reflect that balance.

Enduringly popular
From *The Good Food Guide 1971*: 'superbly cooked dishes', to the 1988 edition: 'nowhere else is it possible to find a well-defined cuisine being practised in such breadth and range ... Some of the sauces are elastically deep'; and the 2011 edition: 'Le Gavroche is like a peerless old stage actor, probably titled, venerable ... still able to exude effortless class as the occasion demands' – Le Gavroche remains a resolutely popular mainstay of the Guide.

Le Gavroche | 43 Upper Brook Street, Mayfair, London W1K 7QR
(020) 7408 0881 | **www.le-gavroche.co.uk**

'The British public's knowledge of French food has gone through an unbelievable transformation over the last 20 years.'

Roast woodcock with grapes and marc
Michel Roux Jr

SERVES 6

FOR THE GAME STOCK

2kg game bones (rabbit, mallard, venison – alternatively, buy a wild rabbit and an old cock pheasant)
1 calf's foot, split
Olive oil, for cooking
1 onion, peeled and roughly chopped
1 carrot, peeled and roughly chopped
2 celery sticks, roughly chopped
6 juniper berries, crushed

FOR THE WOODCOCK

6 woodcock
2 chicken livers, chopped
60g duck foie gras, deveined and chopped
4 shallots, peeled and finely chopped
Sprig of thyme
Olive oil, for cooking
Salt and freshly ground black pepper
1 tbsp brandy
30 white seedless grapes
1 tbsp marc (or grappa)
1 tbsp caster sugar
80g butter, plus 1½ tbsp
6 slices from a loaf of brioche, 5cm square
Sherry vinegar

TO SERVE

Roast potatoes
Lightly steamed carrots
Watercress

1 To make the stock, preheat the oven to 220°C/Gas 7. Put the game bones and calf's foot in a roasting tin with a little olive oil and roast for 15–20 minutes or until well browned. Transfer to a deep, large saucepan and cover with water. Put the onion, carrot and celery into the roasting tin and roast for 5–10 minutes or until brown, then add to the saucepan with the bones.

2 Put the roasting tin over a high heat, add 1 litre of cold water and scrape the bottom with a wooden spatula to loosen the caramelised sugars. Bring to the boil, then pour into the saucepan with the bones and add the juniper berries. Bring to the boil, reduce the heat and simmer for 2 hours, occasionally skimming off the fat and scum that come to the surface. Pass through a sieve and chill. For this recipe you will need 500ml of the stock. Keep the rest in the fridge for up to 7 days or freeze it.

3 To prepare the woodcock, remove the innards from each game bird. Then remove the gizzard by pressing the innards with your fingers. Discard the gizzard, eyes and tongue, which are bitter.

4 Chop the innards, put in a bowl and add the chicken livers, foie gras, 2 of the shallots and the thyme. Heat a frying pan with a drop of oil until smoking. Add the liver mixture and cook over a high heat for just under 1 minute, turning frequently. Season and then flambé with the brandy. Press through a coarse sieve while still hot, mix well with a whisk to emulsify. Allow to cool and keep in the fridge.

5 Blanch the grapes in boiling water for 10 seconds; refresh in cold water, then peel with a small knife. Marinate in the marc and sugar for at least 1 hour.

6 Preheat the oven again to 220°C/Gas 7. Put the birds in a roasting tin with a little oil and sear on all sides over a high heat until evenly browned. Add the 80g of butter and place in the oven to cook for 3 minutes on each side and 4 minutes on their backs. Leave to rest on a rack in a warm place for 15 minutes. Reduce the oven temperature to 180°C/Gas 4.

7 Toast the brioche on both sides, then spread the liver paste over them. Reheat in the oven for 5 minutes before serving.

8 Remove the fat from the roasting tin and add ½ tbsp of butter to the liquid with the remaining shallots. Cook for 2 minutes and then pour in the grapes' marinade and reduce by half. Add 500ml of the game stock (freezing the rest, if not previously frozen) and boil to reduce until lightly thickened. Whisk in 1 tbsp of butter, and reheat the grapes in the sauce at the last moment. A few drops of sherry vinegar will bring out the sweet/sour freshness of this sauce. Serve each woodcock with a slice of brioche topped with liver paste and the roast potatoes, carrots and watercress.

BRYAN WEBB
TYDDYN LLAN

At one time, it was the ambition of most chefs working in the sticks to head for London hoping to make a splash in the biggest pond of all. Bryan Webb undertook that journey in reverse in 2002, waving farewell to a much-lauded operation, Hilaire, on the Old Brompton Road, and returning to his native Wales. The intention had been to open a gastropub in south Wales, but Tyddyn Llan – a compact but beautiful greystone Georgian house near Llandrillo – is some way off that, both geographically and stylistically. Rated as Readers' Restaurant of the Year in Wales in *The Good Food Guide 2010*, and firmly established as the principality's premier gastronomic destination, the building is a pleasing backdrop for Webb's understated but supremely accomplished cooking.

That kind of reputation draws diners from far and wide, but there is also a strong local following. They come back repeatedly for the fine regional lamb, black beef, and seafood from the north Wales boats. His local rabbit with black pudding (see overleaf) may look simple but it has great impact – an emblematic Bryan Webb dish.

'Having cooked in London for 14 years, I felt I had followed all the trends. Now I'm happy just to cook a great piece of beef, perhaps served au poivre, with chips.'

Tyddyn Llan | Llandrillo, near Corwen, Denbighshire LL21 0ST
(01490) 440264 | **www.tyddynllan.co.uk**

Leg of rabbit with black pudding, Carmarthen ham and mustard sauce

Bryan Webb

SERVES 4

4 legs of local rabbits
50g butter
1 tbsp chopped tarragon
120g black pudding
8 slices Carmarthen (or Parma) ham
Olive oil, for cooking
2 shallots, peeled and sliced
150ml white wine
150ml chicken stock
150ml double cream
1 tbsp Dijon mustard

TO SERVE
Mashed potato
Steamed spinach

1 Turn each rabbit leg inside out so that you can remove — and reserve — the thigh bone. Mix the butter and tarragon in a small bowl and divide between the resulting cavity in each leg. Cut the black pudding into 4 slices and put a piece into each leg. Fold the meat around the pudding to re-form the leg.

2 Lay 2 slices of the ham onto a sheet of cling film, place a rabbit leg on top and wrap the ham around the leg. Then wrap in cling film until required. Repeat with the remaining legs.

3 Chop the bones and fry in a little olive oil with the shallots. Add the white wine, bring to the boil and then reduce by half. Add the chicken stock and boil again until only half is left, then add the cream and reduce to a thick, silky sauce. Finally, add the mustard and strain though a fine sieve.

4 Preheat the oven to 200°C/Gas 6. In a non-stick frying pan heat a little olive oil and add the rabbit legs. Cook over a high heat for 1 minute to brown on all sides and then transfer to a roasting tin, pour over any sauce left in the pan and place in the oven for 6 minutes to roast. Turn the legs over and continue to roast for another 6 minutes or until cooked through.

5 Remove the legs from the oven and leave to rest in a warm place for 5–10 minutes.

6 To serve, reheat the sauce and divide between 4 warmed plates. Add spoonfuls of a good creamy mash and spinach and top with the rabbit legs.

'Rabbit is a very versatile meat, full of flavour, and is always a very popular dish on our menus.'

'We try to utilise the harvest around us, from leaves from the garden to Lyth Valley damsons and roe deer from shoots around the area. Some dishes represent just a little corner of Lancashire.'

NIGEL HAWORTH
NORTHCOTE

Think Lancashire food and, even without his star turns on the BBC's *Great British Menu*, you'd think Nigel Haworth. The Accrington-born chef has been at the helm at Northcote, formerly Northcote Manor, since the mid 1980s, steering the kitchen towards only foods produced in the county and bringing such wonders as Lancashire cheese and Morecambe Bay shrimps to culinary attention. Stasis is not an option, though: the dining room has just been refurbished and *The Good Food Guide* praises Northcote's constantly developing menu as well as the restaurant's excellent service.

The hotel boasts an enviable location bordering some wonderful and little-known scenery, but when darkness falls, the emphasis is on well-balanced, feel-good dishes expertly matched with wine from the cellar over which Haworth's business partner, Craig Bancroft, presides.

Northcote | Northcote Road, Langho, Lancashire BB6 8BE
(01254) 240555 | **www.northcote.com**

Festival of food and wine
It is testament to Haworth and Bancroft's reputation in the industry that, since 2001, they've been able to pack Northcote's annual food and drink festival with so many brilliant names. Pierre Koffmann, Raymond Blanc and Michel Roux Jr have all participated, and Philip Howard of The Square has attended every year. Haworth is nevertheless loath to forget his network of suppliers; at last year's event, the top table was shared by Angela Hartnett, a selection of local football dignitaries, and the farmers who grow carrots and cauliflowers for the Northcote kitchen.

Venison carpaccio with mushroom pâté, pickled damsons and hazelnuts

Nigel Haworth

SERVES 4

**FOR THE PICKLED DAMSONS
(MAKE 2 WEEKS AHEAD)**
225g damsons
110g caster sugar
1 cinnamon stick
3 cloves
10g fresh root ginger, peeled and sliced
150ml white wine vinegar

FOR THE VENISON
400g piece of venison cushion (topside)

FOR THE MUSHROOM PÂTÉ
100g button mushrooms, sliced
25g shallots, peeled and finely sliced
1 tbsp olive oil
½ garlic clove, peeled and crushed
Salt and freshly ground black pepper

FOR THE TARRAGON PESTO
50g snipped tarragon
10g pine nuts, roasted
1 garlic clove, peeled and finely chopped
150ml olive oil
60g Parmesan cheese, grated

FOR THE HORSERADISH CREAM
50g crème fraîche
20g horseradish sauce
25g whipping cream, semi-whipped
Pinch of cayenne pepper

TO SERVE
100g white bread dough
Few drops of lemon olive oil
20g peeled and finely diced red onion
8 hazelnuts, roasted and halved
4 caper berries and salad leaves

Specific equipment: see page 259

1 For the pickled damsons, preheat the oven to 140°C/Gas 1. Prick the skins with a needle to prevent them splitting, then put into an ovenproof dish and sprinkle with the sugar. Scatter over the cinnamon, cloves and ginger and cover with the vinegar. Put at the bottom of the oven and cook for about 20 minutes or until the damsons begin to feel soft. Set aside to cool, then strain the juice into a pan, boil for 5 minutes and pour back over the damsons. Put them into a clean jar. They are best kept for 2 weeks before use.

2 Prepare the venison by removing the silverskin and trimming the meat. Lightly roll the venison cushion in cling film and place in the fridge. Once chilled, remove from the fridge and cut 5mm off each end to form a rectangle 11cm long and 6cm wide, then cut into 12 small slices. To turn them into carpaccio slices, place each piece of venison between two polythene bags and bash gently with a meat hammer or rolling pin until they are very thin.

3 To make the pâté, sweat the mushrooms and shallots in the olive oil in a pan for 2–3 minutes or until soft, add the garlic and season with salt and pepper. Cook for a further 8–10 minutes or until all the liquid has evaporated. Put in a food processor and blitz to a rustic pâté. Check the seasoning, transfer to a bowl and set aside.

4 For the pesto, place all the ingredients in a blender and purée well. Transfer to a bowl, check the seasoning and set aside.

5 For the horseradish cream, mix together the crème fraîche and horseradish sauce. Pass the mix through a fine sieve into a bowl, then fold in the cream and season with salt and cayenne pepper. Put into a piping bag.

6 To make bread wafers, preheat the oven to 190°C/Gas 5. Roll the dough through a pasta machine, working down the numbers to number one, dusting the dough lightly with flour to prevent it from sticking. If you don't have a pasta machine, roll as thinly as you can. Lay the dough flat on a dusted worktop. Cut into rectangles measuring 16 x 2.5cm, place on a metal rack and season before baking in the oven for 8–10 minutes or until golden. Remove from the oven, leave to cool then transfer to a plate.

7 To serve, spread 3 slices of venison on each plate and lightly brush with the lemon olive oil and season with salt. Top each bread wafer with 2 small tsp of mushroom pâté and a little horseradish cream. Also put 2 small tsp of pâté on the venison and pipe on 6 tiny cones of horseradish cream. Scatter around the diced red onion, roasted hazelnuts, a caper berry and 2 pickled damsons, cut in half and pitted. Add a bread wafer and finish with the tarragon pesto and salad leaves.

GORDON RAMSAY
RESTAURANT GORDON RAMSAY

Gordon Ramsay has towered over the UK restaurant scene like a colossus for almost two decades. That 'exuberant newcomer', as *The Good Food Guide 1995* described him, has drawn massive press coverage from the start. Ramsay's very French, very refined cooking has a strong classical foundation, his background taking in the culinary giants of the late 20th century – Joël Robuchon and Guy Savoy in Paris, and Albert Roux in London – which also explains Ramsay's fanatical attention to detail.

'Even after 20 years in the industry I'm still learning, and that is what is so exciting. There is always something just round the corner waiting to be discovered.'

It's true that Ramsay's food doesn't take too many risks; it's as haute as cuisine comes and you won't have your senses jarred by oddball pairings. But, while dishes are honed to technical perfection, they have an exquisite quality about them. Perhaps his true genius is as a consummate restaurateur with his restaurant at Royal Hospital Road, his treasured London flagship, a consistent top scorer in the Guide for the last decade.

Restaurant Gordon Ramsay | 68 Royal Hospital Road, Chelsea, London SW3 4HP
(020) 7352 4441 | **www.gordonramsay.com**

Roasted loin of venison with braised red cabbage, parsnip chips and parsnip purée

Gordon Ramsay

SERVES 4

FOR THE BRAISED RED CABBAGE

1 small red cabbage
100g butter
150g light soft brown sugar
75ml sherry or red wine vinegar

FOR THE PARSNIP PURÉE

2 parsnips
150ml milk
75ml double cream
25g butter
Sea salt and freshly ground black pepper

FOR THE BEETROOT FONDANT

2 beetroot
15g butter, plus a few knobs
1 tsp olive oil
100ml vegetable or chicken stock

FOR THE PARSNIP CRISPS

2 parsnips
Groundnut oil, for deep-frying

FOR THE RED WINE SAUCE

3 banana shallots, peeled and finely chopped
2 tbsp olive oil

About 200g or more meat trimmings (from beef, veal or poultry)
½ tsp black peppercorns
Few sprigs of thyme
1 bay leaf
1 tbsp sherry or red wine vinegar
750ml red wine
400ml chicken stock
400ml veal stock

FOR THE VENISON

600g loin of venison
1½ tbsp olive oil, plus extra for drizzling
Few knobs of butter

1 For the braised red cabbage, halve the cabbage, cut out the tough core and finely shred the leaves. Heat the butter, sugar and vinegar in a saucepan. When the butter has melted and the sugar dissolved, tip in the cabbage and stir well to coat. Place a crumpled piece of greaseproof paper on top of the cabbage and cook over a low heat on the hob for about 1½ hours or until the cabbage is tender. Lift the greaseproof paper and give the cabbage a stir every once in a while. If there is still a fair amount of liquid in the cabbage when it's cooked, strain the cabbage and boil the liquid until reduced to a syrupy sauce. Pour the sauce back over the cabbage and toss to coat, then set aside.

2 For the parsnip purée, peel the parsnips and finely slice the thinner ends. Cut the thicker ends into quarters, removing the tough cores, and thinly slice. Place them in a saucepan with the milk and cook for 20–25 minutes or until very soft. Tip the cooked parsnips and milk into a blender and whiz to a purée. Return to the pan and stir in the cream and butter. Season to taste with salt and pepper. Transfer to a squeezy bottle and keep warm in a pan of hot water.

3 For the beetroot fondant, peel the beetroot and cut into 1.5cm-thick rounds. If you like, cut out perfect rounds using metal pastry cutters. Heat the 15g of butter and the olive oil in a frying pan. Season the beetroot rounds and fry on a high heat for about 2 minutes on each side or until browned. Pour in the stock and bring to the boil. Dot the beetroot with tiny knobs of butter then put a piece of greaseproof paper on top. Reduce the heat and simmer gently for 10–15 minutes or until most of the stock has been absorbed and the beetroot is tender. Keep warm.

4 To make the parsnip crisps, peel and finely slice the parsnips into ribbons with a swivel vegetable peeler. Heat the groundnut oil in a deep saucepan or deep-fat fryer until hot and a small piece of bread dropped into the hot oil sizzles. Fry the parsnip ribbons in batches until golden brown. Drain on kitchen paper and sprinkle with sea salt. Keep warm in a low oven.

5 To make the red wine sauce, sauté the shallots with the olive oil in a wide heavy-based saucepan for 4–6 minutes or until they are soft and begin to caramelise. Add the meat trimmings and fry for a few more minutes or until the meat is browned. Add the peppercorns, thyme, bay leaf and vinegar. Deglaze the pan with the red wine and bring it to the boil. Boil rapidly until reduced by three quarters to a rich syrupy glaze. Add the chicken and veal stocks and return to the boil. Once again, boil vigorously until the sauce has reduced by half or until it has reached a desired consistency. Strain it through a fine sieve and season to taste. Reheat before serving.

6 When ready to serve, preheat the oven to 200°C/Gas 6. Season the venison with salt and pepper. Heat the olive oil in an ovenproof frying pan and sear the venison on a high heat for 4–5 minutes, turning frequently until browned all over. Add the butter and, as it melts and foams, spoon it over the venison to baste. Put the pan into the oven and roast the venison for 6–8 minutes or until it is medium rare. It should feel lightly springy when pressed. Remove and leave to rest for a few minutes while you reheat the red wine sauce.

7 To serve, put a neat pile of braised red cabbage onto the centre of each warmed plate. Put a beetroot fondant on top and squeeze little dots of parsnip purée around the edge of the plates. Slice the venison thickly and overlap the slices in a small mound on top of the beetroot. Pour the red wine sauce around the plate and drizzle with a little olive oil. Finally, garnish each plate with the parsnip crisps and serve at once.

PHILIP HOWARD
THE SQUARE

Of all the classic virtues we hope to find in a restaurant – whether we're off to the local tandoori on a Friday night, or living it large in London's West End – the greatest is consistency. It is a quality that has underpinned Philip Howard's two decades at The Square. From its earliest days on St James's Square to its present home within a nightingale's tweet of Berkeley Square, this has been one of the capital's culinary hot-spots.

'I've never really been motivated by the desire to be innovative or different,' Howard says. 'I have incorporated some of the newer trends, but in a way that I hope dovetails successfully with the classical technique that informs 95 per cent of what I do.' It all takes place in a generously proportioned, smart but not intimidating room hung with vivid modern paintings, a venue reliably packed throughout the week.

It may be hard to showcase regional produce in the heart of Mayfair, but Howard has always been proud of the fact that the vast majority of what finds its way onto the expansive Square menus is British. Indeed, he isn't averse to gathering elderflowers and nettles around his southwest London home when the season delivers them. And barely any season is more eagerly anticipated than the two spring months when British lamb is at its eloquent, luxurious best.

The Square | 6–10 Bruton Street, Mayfair, London W1J 6PU
(020) 7495 7100 | **www.squarerestaurant.com**

'**What brings people back to The Square is the desire to eat lovely things. I've always cooked food that I enjoy eating. Food that you don't have to worry about understanding. When a dish is right, it's delicious. That's all that matters.'**

Herb-crusted saddle of lamb with shallot purée and rosemary
Philip Howard

SERVES 6

1 saddle of lamb weighing about 2kg, off the bone with the outer husk removed and 2 small fillets reserved

FOR THE HERB CRUST

100g breadcrumbs

1 tbsp grated Parmesan cheese

1 tbsp mixed finely chopped parsley, rosemary and thyme

Salt and freshly ground black pepper

1 garlic clove, peeled

100g butter, melted

1 small egg

FOR THE ACCOMPANIMENTS

3 small waxy potatoes, left unpeeled

175g butter

12 garlic cloves, peeled

Sprig of thyme

250g spinach

3 cooked artichoke hearts, halved

3 cooked peppers, cut into strips

25ml olive oil

FOR THE SHALLOT PURÉE

20 shallots, peeled and thinly sliced

50g butter

100ml double cream

FOR THE SAUCE

50ml lamb stock

Sprig of rosemary

25ml olive oil

2 tomatoes, blanched, peeled, deseeded and diced

1 Lay the saddle of lamb out on a chopping board with the two 'loins' of meat running parallel away from you. Trim off all the fatty meat on either side of the loins, leaving you a rectangular piece about 20 x 15cm. Insert the two fillets between the two loins and leave the meat to sit like this in the fridge overnight.

2 For the herb crust, place the dry ingredients and garlic in a food processor and blend for 30 seconds. Gradually add the melted butter and, finally, the egg. Roll this paste out between 2 sheets of greaseproof paper with a rolling pin until 2mm thick and place in the fridge to chill and set.

3 When you are ready to cook, preheat the oven to 220°C/Gas 6.

4 To cook the potatoes, trim the ends off each potato and cut in half lengthways. Season and gently cook in a saucepan in 100g of the butter for 10–15 minutes on each side or until golden.

5 About an hour before you wish to eat, season the lamb on the fat and meat sides and brown the fat sides on a medium heat in a heavy-based roasting tin. Baste the meat with the rendered fat and then roast in the oven for 15–20 minutes (15 minutes for rare and 20 minutes for medium). Remove from the oven.

6 Place the garlic cloves with 25g of the butter and the thyme in a roasting tin and cook in the oven for 15–20 minutes or until soft.

7 Take the herb crust out of the fridge and cut out a rectangle to fit the lamb. Peel off one layer of greaseproof paper and place the crust over the non-fat side of the lamb. Peel off the second layer of greaseproof paper and leave the crust to melt into the lamb while it rests for 20 minutes.

8 Meanwhile, make the shallot purée. Sweat the shallots in a saucepan in of the butter with a good pinch of salt and pepper. Once softened, add the cream and bring to the boil, then purée in a blender. Pass through a fine sieve into a clean pan and keep warm.

9 Cook the spinach in the remaining 50g of butter with pepper and salt for about 1 minute or until wilted and drain well. Sauté the artichokes and peppers in the olive oil.

10 To finish the lamb, preheat the grill to hot. Place the lamb under the grill for 2–3 minutes or until browned.

11 Just prior to serving, make the sauce. Bring the lamb stock to the boil, add the rosemary and olive oil and the diced tomatoes and cook for a few minutes before straining.

12 Carve the lamb into thick slices and serve one slice on each warmed plate on a spoonful of spinach together with the roasted garlic, potatoes, sautéed artichokes and peppers and the shallot purée. Pour the sauce around the meat and serve at once.

'This has been one of my half-dozen signature dishes over the last 20 years. There's hardly anything to compare with the flavour and tenderness of spring lamb.'

'The most important thing to me is clear flavours, clean presentation and making sure we are using first-rate seasonal produce.'

DOMINIC CHAPMAN
THE ROYAL OAK

The son of hoteliers, Dominic Chapman cites childhood trips around France and Greece with his parents as his earliest introduction to good food. Despite coming from a family immersed in hospitality and catering (his parents own The Castle at Taunton), it was never his intention to become a chef. After school, he went travelling 'to avoid the catering business', but it was on his travels in New Zealand that he spotted the second volume of his father Kit's book, *Great British Chefs*. He then used this to find his first jobs on his return to London, including an influential spell under Rowley Leigh at Kensington Place.

Chapman's big break was when Heston Blumenthal appointed him head chef of his Hind's Head pub in Bray then, in 2007, he moved across Berkshire to The Royal Oak at Paley Street, a smart country pub owned by Sir Michael Parkinson. With its open fire, beams and leather sofas, it is the perfect platform for Chapman's simple British cooking – classics such as Lancashire hotpot, smoked eel with beetroot and horseradish, and rhubarb trifle – and he was named Best Pub Chef in *The Good Food Guide 2009*. Letting well-sourced ingredients speak for themselves is Chapman's philosophy, but, he says, just because it's a pub, there's no excuse for sloppy presentation: 'If people are paying good money, they should be able to see that the chef has taken a lot of care in preparation.'

The Royal Oak | Paley Street, Berkshire SL6 3JN
(01628) 620541 | **www.theroyaloakpaleystreet.com**

Oxtail and kidney pie
Dominic Chapman

MAKES 6 INDIVIDUAL PIES

FOR THE ONIONS AND MUSHROOMS

100g butter

350g peeled and sliced onions

150g meaty mushrooms, such as button, wood blewits, horse, quartered

FOR THE OXTAIL

1kg oxtail on the bone

2 tbsp seasoned plain flour

Olive oil, for cooking

100g pancetta

2 knobs of butter

20g peeled and sliced onion

20g peeled and chopped carrot

20g trimmed and chopped leek

20g chopped celery

1 garlic clove, peeled and chopped

50g button mushrooms

2 small tomatoes

250ml port

250ml Madeira wine

250ml red wine

500ml chicken stock

500ml veal or chicken stock

1 tsp chopped thyme

1 bay leaf

4g pink and white peppercorns

Salt and freshly ground black pepper

Squeeze of lemon juice

FOR THE HAM HOCK

1kg ham hock

50g peeled and chopped carrot

50g trimmed and chopped leek

50g chopped celery

50g peeled and chopped onion

2 garlic cloves, peeled and chopped

5g thyme leaves

1 bay leaf

FOR THE KIDNEY

½ veal kidney

3 garlic cloves, peeled

1 tsp chopped thyme

1 bay leaf

FOR THE PIE TOP PASTRY

200g suet

400g self-raising flour

1 egg yolk

Specific equipment: see page 259

1 To cook the onions, melt the butter in a pan, add the onions and leave them to cook without browning on a low heat for about 4 hours or until they are completely soft, turning them every once in a while to prevent them catching. Drain off excess butter into another pan and store the onions in the fridge until required. Fry the mushrooms in the butter from the onions for about 5 minutes or until golden brown. Drain off excess butter and set the mushrooms aside until required.

2 Roll the oxtail in the seasoned flour and then brown on all sides in 1 tbsp of olive oil in a large pan. Once evenly caramelised (coloured but not burnt), set aside in a casserole dish. Brown the pancetta in the same pan then also add to the casserole dish. Add a little more oil and the butter to the pan and caramelise the onion, carrot, leek, celery and garlic. In a separate pan caramelise the mushrooms in butter and oil. Add all the vegetables to the casserole dish.

3 Preheat the oven to 180°C/Gas 4. Cut the tomatoes in half and place flat side down on a baking tray with a little water. Place in the oven and roast for about 10 minutes or until soft and caramelised. Add to the casserole dish. Reduce the oven temperature to 100°C/Gas ¼.

4 Deglaze the pan with the port and Madeira and reduce by half. Then add the red wine and again reduce by half and add to the casserole dish. Add the two stocks, cover the casserole dish with foil and place in the oven for 3 hours or until tender. Remove the dish from the oven and, once cool enough to handle, pass the stock through a fine sieve. Reserve the meat but throw away the vegetables. Pick all the meat from the oxtail (leave the pieces fairly large), and cut the pancetta into bite-sized pieces. Reduce the stock in the pan until it's the consistency of rich gravy, and then add the herbs, seasoning and lemon juice. Pass through the fine sieve again.

5 Place the ham hock in a large saucepan of cold water and bring to the boil, then rinse for 5 minutes under cold water. Return the ham hock to the pan, cover with cold water, add all the

other ingredients and simmer for 2 hours or until tender. Remove the hock from the stock, pick off all the meat, cut into bite-sized pieces and keep on one side until required.

6 For the kidney, remove all fat from the kidney and cut into bite-sized pieces. Place in a pan of cold water and bring to the boil, then rinse for 5 minutes under cold water. Place in a clean pan, cover with cold water and then add the garlic, thyme and bay leaf and simmer for 1½ hours or until tender. Let the kidney cool in the stock.

7 To make the pastry, mix together the suet, flour and a pinch of salt in a bowl. Carefully add enough cold water to achieve a firm dough. Rest the dough in the fridge for 1 hour before use.

8 Season each element of the pie then place the following quantity of each ingredient into each of six 500ml pie dishes: 90g oxtail, 25g kidney pieces (drained from the stock), 10g pancetta, 25g ham hock, 5g mushrooms, 20g melted onions, 120g sauce.

9 Roll out six 100g balls of pastry into 15cm-diameter circles, place over the pie dishes and crimp around the edges. Trim the edges with a knife and make a small cross in the centre of each with the tip of a knife. Leave to rest in the fridge for about 20 minutes and preheat the oven to 200°C/ Gas 6. Mix together the egg yolk with a little water and brush the egg wash over the pastry before placing in the oven. Cook the pies for 12 minutes or until golden brown and serve immediately.

'Our menu follows the seasons and pays homage to an array of fantastic food producers – what I love about cooking is the potential to inspire and excite.'

LAURIE GEAR
ARTICHOKE

A restaurant called Artichoke begs an obvious question – why the name? 'No special reason,' Gear laughs. It was more a moment of serendipity that happened when, in 2002, he first acquired what had formerly been a vegetarian place. He found an old bit of panel with a globe artichoke painted on it and the name seemed to express a certain quirkiness.

Having cooked at Noma in Copenhagen and also for the glitterati at Pinewood Studios, Gear has had a wider-ranging tutelage than many. That is reflected in a versatile approach that blends elements of English and French styles while harking back to the simple Cornish fish dishes that one of his earliest employers specialised in. Local farmers are enthusiastically supported as much as possible, with a sense of commitment derived in part from wife and partner Jacqueline's own Devon farming lineage.

The creativity and ambition going on at Artichoke makes it feel like a pint pot out of which a bounteous quart of good things is somehow being poured, and has earned it the Editors' Award for Best New Entry in *The Good Food Guide 2011* following fire damage in 2008, which had meant a long closure for the restaurant. Indeed, the menu never stands still. 'I like to ring the changes,' says its chef-patron, to which a dish of meltingly tender beef accompanied by a watercress sauce (see overleaf) bears witness.

Artichoke | 9 Market Square, Old Amersham, Buckinghamshire HP7 0DF
(01494) 726611 | **www.artichokerestaurant.co.uk**

Slow-roasted rib eye of Dedham Vale beef with oxtail croquettes, wet garlic purée and watercress sauce
Laurie Gear

SERVES 4

720g piece of Dedham vale rib eye cut into 4 thick oblong pieces

Vegetable oil, for cooking

Sea salt and freshly ground black pepper

15g butter

FOR THE CROQUETTES

150g plain flour

400g oxtail on the bone, sliced

½ tbsp rapeseed oil

1 banana shallot, peeled and diced

2 garlic cloves, peeled and diced

Sprig of thyme

1 bay leaf

100ml red wine

500ml chicken stock

50ml balsamic vinegar

25g butter

50ml milk

50ml double cream

1 egg and 1 egg yolk, lightly beaten

2 tbsp chopped parsley

FOR THE ACCOMPANIMENTS

2 large waxy potatoes, left unpeeled

65g butter

1 tbsp peeled and grated horseradish

Vegetable oil, for cooking

12 baby beets

12 young carrots, trimmed

2 tbsp chicken stock

Sprig of thyme

1 garlic clove, peeled and sliced

FOR THE WATERCRESS SAUCE

2 large bunches of watercress

1 onion, peeled and finely sliced

1 leek, trimmed and finely sliced

1 celery stick, finely sliced

Vegetable oil, for cooking

1 potato, peeled and finely sliced

400ml chicken stock

FOR THE WET GARLIC PURÉE

3 bulbs of new season wet garlic

50ml double cream, warmed

TO COOK THE CROQUETTES

25g seasoned flour

1 egg, lightly beaten

100g breadcrumbs

Vegetable oil, for cooking

1 Seal the rib eye portions very quickly in a hot pan with vegetable oil, season and roll tightly into sausage shapes. Wrap securely in cling film and tie at both ends. Allow to cool and then place the rolls in the fridge for 24 hours to set their shape.

2 For the croquettes, preheat the oven to 160°C/Gas 3. Season 50g of the flour and use it to coat the oxtail pieces. Heat the rapeseed oil in a flameproof casserole dish with a lid and brown the oxtail until golden. Add the shallot, garlic and herbs and sweat for 2–3 minutes to soften.

3 Add the red wine, bring to the boil and then turn down the heat and let the wine reduce by three quarters (4–6 minutes). Add the chicken stock and balsamic vinegar, cover with the lid and cook in the oven for about 2½ hours or until the oxtail is tender. Remove the dish from the oven and the oxtail from the liquid and pick off the meat from the bone. Cut the meat into shreds. Strain the remaining liquor into a clean pan and reduce on the hob until it is thick and syrupy.

4 In a heavy-based saucepan, melt the butter and add the remaining flour to form a roux. Cook it over a low heat for 4–6 minutes or until golden brown and then add the milk and cream and stir until thick. Add the reduced oxtail liquid, then remove the pan from the heat and stir in the beaten egg. Fold in the shredded oxtail meat and add the parsley. Let the mixture cool.

5 Line a baking tray with baking parchment. Place the oxtail mixture into a piping bag fitted with a plain wide nozzle and pipe out 4 finger-sized lengths of croquette mixture onto the tray. Leave to set in the refrigerator for 3–4 hours.

6 When you are ready to cook the dish, heat a saucepan of water to 60°C, put the wrapped rib eye rolls into it and cook for 1 hour, checking the heat remains at 60°C. Preheat the oven to 180°C/Gas 4. Finely slice the potatoes on a mandoline or using a very sharp knife and arrange on a baking sheet to make 4 potato 'cakes' each with 8 overlapping slices. Melt 50g of the butter with the horseradish and brush over the slices. In a hot frying pan, heat 1 tsp vegetable oil and brown the slices on both sides, return to the baking sheet and then cook in the oven for about 5 minutes or until soft. Season and trim the edges to serve. Keep in a warm place. Wrap the baby beets in foil and roast for 30–40 minutes.

7 To make the watercress sauce, trim the watercress and blanch in boiling salted water for 2 minutes, then plunge into iced water. Sweat the onion, leek and celery in a little vegetable oil in a saucepan. Add the sliced potato and chicken stock and cook for about 10 minutes or until the potato is soft. Purée in a blender. Then allow to cool slightly, add the watercress and purée again. Pass through a fine sieve and season to taste. Keep warm.

8 For the wet garlic purée, break the garlic into cloves and plunge in boiling water for 2 minutes. Drain the water and repeat this process with fresh boiling water a further 3 times, adding a little salt to the last batch of water. Purée the hot strained garlic cloves with the warmed cream in a blender, pass through a fine sieve and season to taste. Keep warm.

9 Roll the oxtail croquettes in the seasoned flour, then the egg and then the breadcrumbs until evenly coated. Heat the vegetable oil in a deep-fat fryer to 175°C and cook the croquettes for about 3 minutes or until golden. Drain on kitchen paper and keep warm.

10 Cook the carrots in the remaining butter and the 2 tbsp of stock for 5 minutes or until soft.

11 Remove the rib eye rolls from the hot water and take off the cling film. Melt the butter in a hot pan and quickly brown the rolls, adding seasoning, the thyme and garlic.

12 To serve, spoon the watercress sauce across 4 warmed plates and cover each with a potato slice. Slice the rib eye rolls and arrange on each potato slice. Spoon across a little warm wet garlic purée and then add a croquette and the vegetables.

'We try to buy the best produce available, and then all the work is in the preparation and the cooking. We're a country pub with a local butcher – we can see the animals walking around on the hillside.'

MICHAEL NORTH
THE NUT TREE INN

You can't get meat more traceable than pigs reared in what is effectively the back garden, so it's no wonder that The Nut Tree Inn won the award for Best Use of Local Produce in *The Good Food Guide 2010*. Michael North and his wife Imogen bought their pretty thatched pub in 2006 – previously, he was head chef at The Goose at Britwell Salome – and they proceeded to set out their stall with a menu featuring their own sausages.

North makes no claim to be a smallholder himself, but he discusses his pigs with the easy confidence of someone who is happy both to raise animals and send them to slaughter. 'We have five pigs ready to go to the abattoir at the moment,' he says. 'We use the ears and tail and head and trotters, the whole caboodle.'

Keeping it simple

The steak and chips recipe (see overleaf) reflects Michael North's conviction that a pub should be a pub, complete with big, hearty dishes and comfortable corners in which to have a pint. But his food by no means lacks ambition, and what *The Good Food Guide* praises as an 'exact and assured' approach is clear in dishes such as a pavé of local venison with butternut squash purée and bourguignon sauce, or a ballotine of foie gras offset with the clean acidity of poached rhubarb.

The Nut Tree Inn | Main Street, Murcott, Oxfordshire OX5 2RE
(01865) 331253 | **www.nuttreeinn.co.uk**

Grilled fillet of aged beef with triple-cooked chips, onion rings, baked tomato and tarragon butter
Michael North

SERVES 4

4 large vine plum tomatoes

Olive oil, for cooking

Salt and freshly ground black pepper

4 large Maris Piper potatoes, peeled and cut into even-sized chips

4 fillet steaks, about 200–250g each and preferably dry-aged for 28 days

Unsalted butter, for cooking

FOR THE TARRAGON BUTTER

Bunch of young tarragon, finely chopped

125g unsalted butter, softened

FOR THE ONION RINGS

100g cornflour

150g plain flour, plus extra for dusting

½ tsp baking powder

600ml soda water

1 large Spanish onion, peeled and cut into rings

1 Preheat the oven to 200°C/Gas 6. Trim the base of each tomato, so they can stand alone, keeping a small piece of the vine intact. Lightly dress in olive oil, season and then bake for about 20 minutes or until tender and lightly browned.

2 Put the chips into a large saucepan, cover with salted water and bring to the boil. Continue to boil for 3–4 minutes or until cooked and fluffy but still holding their shape. Drain the chips and lay flat on a rack to dry, cool and form a skin.

3 Heat a deep-fat fryer to 140°C and blanch the chips in the oil for 2–3 minutes or until pale gold, then remove to the cooling rack again. Leave to dry, cool and form a skin.

4 For the tarragon butter, mix the chopped tarragon with the butter. Roll in greaseproof paper to form a cylinder and leave to chill in the fridge.

5 For the onion rings, combine the cornflour, plain flour and baking powder and whisk in the soda water to form a light airy batter. Season with salt. Select 3 onion rings per portion (totalling 12 rings). Dust with flour and submerge in the batter. Set aside.

6 For the beef, heat a large frying pan until almost smoking. Season the steaks with salt and pepper. Add a small amount of olive oil to the pan and seal the steaks on each side over a high heat. Reduce the heat, add a large knob of unsalted butter and cook for about 6 minutes (rare), 10 minutes (medium) or 14 minutes (well-done), basting and turning the steaks constantly. Remove from the pan and leave to rest while cooking the chips and onion rings.

7 Heat the deep-fat fryer to 170°C. Drain the onion rings from the batter and add to the fryer together with the chips and fry for 5–6 minutes or until golden and crunchy.

8 To serve, place 1 tomato and 1 steak on each warmed plate along with the chips. Slice the tarragon butter, removing the paper, and place a piece on top of each steak. Add 3 onion rings to each and serve.

'We like to have a certain number of pub classics on the menu as well as more restaurant-style dishes.'

Desserts

'I liked the fact that I had to build my reputation from scratch here in Edinburgh. There were no expectations, and people gradually came to realise I could cook.'

TOM KITCHIN
THE KITCHIN

Regenerated dockland areas became the mood of the moment in 1990s Britain, but it's fair to say some have been more successful than others. Tom Kitchin recalls that, when he opened his self-named restaurant in the Leith development in Edinburgh, there was a hint of the ghost town about the place. What are now his premises had seen a fair few restaurants fail before him, so the stakes were high.

He enjoys the fact that nobody had the faintest idea who he was in those days, but Kitchin can be forgiven that little chuckle for he's come a long way since he began as a teenager. After working for the great Pierre Koffmann at La Tante Claire, London, he went on to work with Alain Ducasse and Guy Savoy. That's not a bad CV for an Edinburgh lad to have in his back pocket on his return home.

The Kitchin is a cool, contemporary venue, where the light is filtered through slatted blinds and the kitchen brigade is partially open to view. Those training years were not wasted. Kitchin's food is among the best, not just in Scotland, but in the UK. His resonant depth of flavour booms through impeccably conceived modern dishes that are polished to a dazzling sheen with French technique. They all use fine Scottish produce and, for the parfait overleaf, what could be more Scottish than honey from the heathery hillsides of Perthshire?

The Kitchin | 78 Commercial Quay, Leith, Edinburgh EH6 6LX
(0131) 555 1755 | **www.thekitchin.com**

Honey parfait with pickled plums and oat crumble

Tom Kitchin

MAKES 4 INDIVIDUAL PARFAITS

FOR THE HONEY PARFAIT
90g clear honey
4 egg yolks
300ml double cream
1 tsp Drambuie

FOR THE PLUM CRISPS
1 plum, very thinly sliced
50g icing sugar

FOR THE CRUMBLE MIX
50g rolled oats
50g pecans
1 tsp egg white
1 tbsp icing sugar

FOR THE PICKLED PLUMS
300ml red wine
1 tbsp clear honey
3 tsp sugar
75ml white wine vinegar
2 cinnamon sticks
3 cloves
Juice of ½ lemon
6 plums

TO SERVE
1 plum, diced
Mint leaves

Specific equipment: see page 259

1 To make the honey parfait, heat the honey in a small saucepan, bring to the boil and set aside. In a small bowl, whisk the egg yolks until pale and thick, then slowly add the honey to the yolks, whisking until everything is combined.

2 In a separate bowl, whisk the cream to firm peaks and fold in the Drambuie. Fold the honey and egg yolk mixture into the whipped cream and Drambuie. Pour into four 7.5cm-diameter x 5cm-deep (about 150ml) dariole moulds and put in the freezer to set. The parfait keeps for a few days in the freezer, so can be prepared in advance.

3 For the plum crisps, preheat the oven to 100°C/Gas ¼ and line a baking tray with baking parchment. Place the plum slices on the baking tray and dust generously with icing sugar on one side, then turn the slices over and dust the other side. Place in the oven and leave to dry for about 2 hours, then check: if they are not yet crisp, cook for a while longer, but keep checking.

4 When the plums are crisp, remove from the oven and increase the heat to 180°C/Gas 4. Line a second baking tray with baking parchment. Toss all the crumble ingredients together in a bowl and spread out on the tray. Bake for 6–8 minutes or until golden brown. Break up the crumble into smallish chunks and set aside.

5 To prepare the pickled plums, place everything except the plums in a stainless-steel or ceramic pan. Bring to the boil, then take off the heat and leave to infuse for 15 minutes. Strain and leave to cool. Once the pickling liquid has cooled to room temperature, stone and slice the plums into thin discs and steep them in the liquid for at least 1 hour.

6 To serve, arrange a circle of pickled plum slices on each plate. Turn the parfait out onto the plums and then top with a little of the diced plum and the oat crumble. Decorate with mint leaves and plum crisps.

'This is a very simple dessert that uses the kind of product that I'm fanatical about, Heather Hills Farm honey from Perthshire, sourced from hillsides where the grouse feed.'

DAVID EVERITT-MATTHIAS
LE CHAMPIGNON SAUVAGE

David Everitt-Matthias is an intelligent, thoughtful chef, who, with his wife Helen, has long run one of the premier restaurants in the country – Le Champignon Sauvage, listed in *The Good Food Guide* for an impressive 22 years. He has always concentrated on his craft and the kitchen rather than creating a celebrity image for himself, and it shows.

Confident enough to do things his way rather than follow fashion, Everitt-Matthias's highly technical, modern French cookery embraces wild rootsy flavours. A forager's hand is much in evidence in dishes like sorrel ice cream (see overleaf), which is thanks to an aunt ('a wonderful hedgerow cook'), who encouraged her nephew to cook and to learn about wild foods from when he was seven.

'The driving force behind my cooking is always to be happy in what I am doing, to improve any way I can, and to be true to my style.'

He admires Pierre Gagnaire for his 'sheer invention and presentation' and Gordon Ramsay for 'his technique and organisation', but the biggest career influence dates from a *stage* at La Tante Claire and the brilliant Pierre Koffmann with his ability to turn the most humble dish into something wonderful. It's a trick Everitt-Matthias has pulled off with his own restaurant: it may look like an ordinary terraced house on an ordinary busy street but, once inside, you're in a different world.

Le Champignon Sauvage | 24–26 Suffolk Road, Cheltenham, Gloucestershire GL50 2AQ
(01242) 573449 | **www.lechampignonsauvage.co.uk**

Sorrel ice cream with wood sorrel and compote of brambles

David Everitt-Matthias

SERVES 6

FOR THE SORREL ICE CREAM
300ml milk
200ml double cream
6 egg yolks
60g caster sugar
10g milk powder
10ml liquid glucose
7g ascorbic acid
75g sorrel

FOR THE BRAMBLE COMPOTE
750g brambles
100g caster sugar
3g gelatine leaves
Juice of 1 lemon

TO SERVE
25g wood sorrel

1 To make the sorrel ice cream, gently bring the milk and cream to the boil in a large heavy-based saucepan. Meanwhile, in a bowl, whisk the egg yolks with the sugar, milk powder and glucose until pale and creamy.

2 Pour half the milk mixture onto the eggs, whisking to combine, then pour this back into the saucepan. Cook over a gentle heat, stirring constantly with a wooden spoon, until the mixture thickens enough to coat the back of the spoon (it should register about 84°C on a thermometer).

3 Remove from the heat, add the ascorbic acid and sorrel, then transfer to a blender and purée until the sorrel has completely disintegrated and you are left with a vivid green liquid. Strain through a fine sieve into a large bowl and freeze in an ice-cream machine according to the manufacturer's instructions. Transfer to the fridge about 10 minutes before serving to soften slightly.

4 For the bramble compote, lightly cook the brambles with the sugar until the juices just start to run; do not cook them for too long or they will become mushy. Meanwhile, soak the gelatine in cold water for about 5 minutes to soften and then squeeze to drain.

5 Drain the berries gently into a bowl, being careful not to let them break up. Place the juice and 50g of the brambles in a blender and purée until smooth. Add the lemon juice and strain through a fine sieve, pushing through as much of the fruit as you can. Add the gelatine to the purée and stir until dissolved. Leave to cool, then add the remaining brambles.

6 To serve, arrange the brambles on 6 plates and drizzle with a little of the juice. Place a large scoop of sorrel ice cream on each plate and decorate with the wood sorrel.

'We have a lot of sorrel growing not too far from brambles; it seemed natural to pair the acidic leaves with the sweet and deeply musky-flavoured fruit.'

> *'The poached rhubarb in my recipe reminds me of rhubarb and custard sweets. My dad ran a sweet shop, and I used to walk through it on the way to school and rob one. It's a dish associated with the north, but with its classic components rejuvenated.'*

MARC WILKINSON
FRAICHE

Success in food for Marc Wilkinson wasn't inevitable: his early experiences in the kitchen (cooking beans on toast for his brother, followed by a disappointing spell at catering college) were not edifying. But stints at the Chester Grosvenor and Pennyhill Park hotels and the restaurant-with-rooms Winteringham Fields, equipped him well for going it alone on the Wirral, where his father still lives. Hidden away in a conservation village a few miles from Birkenhead, Fraiche is a restaurant that deserves seeking out.

Although Gallic ingredients share a billing with the local produce, Fraiche feels very much of its place and reflects its patron: a locally raised chef doing things in his own, clean-cut modern way. Wilkinson travels to eat whenever he can, and early each year takes the opportunity to close the restaurant and set up a workshop, developing new dishes in relative peace. His rationale is one of constant thought and evolution.

Small but beautiful

Marc Wilkinson's small, serene restaurant with just 14 covers has led the pack on Merseyside since it opened in 2004, and sets an example further afield. Other, showier kitchens could learn much from Wilkinson's ability to innovate and the inspired Sunday night sessions that showcase new ideas in the style of a brilliant comic warming up for the Edinburgh Fringe. The wine selection, awarded Wine List of the Year in *The Good Food Guide 2010*, is equally accessible.

Fraiche | 11 Rose Mount, Oxton, Merseyside CH43 5SG
(0151) 652 2914 | **www.restaurantfraiche.com**

Poached rhubarb with caramelised cream and coconut sorbet
Marc Wilkinson

SERVES 4

FOR THE COCONUT SORBET

500g coconut purée or coconut cream

50g glucose

50g caster sugar

Pinch of citric acid or squeeze of lemon juice

Coconut shards, to decorate

FOR THE SESAME BISCUITS

30g unsalted butter, softened

65g caster sugar

25ml orange juice

35g plain flour

25g sesame seeds

FOR THE CRUMBLE

225g plain flour

175g unsalted butter, diced

85g caster sugar

25g rolled oats, chopped

25g chopped peeled hazelnuts

FOR THE RHUBARB

150g caster sugar

4 rhubarb stalks, trimmed and peeled

Capful of Grenadine

2 slices of fresh root ginger, peeled

2 tbsp cornflour

FOR THE RHUBARB CLOUD

3.5g gold gelatine leaves

25g caster sugar

FOR THE CARAMELISED CREAM

2g gelatine leaves

100ml milk

100ml double cream

1 vanilla pod

1½ egg yolks

20g caster sugar

0.4g agar agar

Light soft brown sugar

Specific equipment: see page 259

1 To prepare the sorbet, put all the ingredients except the coconut shards into a saucepan and heat gently until the glucose and sugar are fully dissolved, then pass through a sieve and allow to cool. Freeze in an ice-cream machine according to the manufacturer's instructions. Keep in the freezer, taking out 15 minutes before serving if it is hard to the touch.

2 To make the sesame biscuits, cream the butter with the sugar until smooth. Add the orange juice and then the flour, mixing until a paste is achieved. Then mix in the sesame seeds and rest in the fridge for about 2 hours to firm up.

3 Preheat the oven to 160°C/Gas 3, spread the sesame mix over a non-stick baking sheet and cook for 5–10 minutes or until golden. Remove from the oven, cut into rectangles and keep in an airtight container. Leave the oven on for the crumble.

4 To make the crumble, put the flour, butter and sugar into a bowl and rub to the consistency of breadcrumbs with your hands. Add the oats and hazelnuts and leave to firm up in the fridge. Spread on a non-stick baking sheet and bake for 8–10 minutes or until golden. Leave to cool then store in an airtight container.

5 For the poached rhubarb, reduce the oven temperature to 120°C/Gas ½. Put the caster sugar with 150ml of water into a saucepan and gently bring to the boil to dissolve the sugar and make a stock syrup. Leave to cool.

6 Meanwhile, cut the rhubarb into 10cm pieces. Transfer the syrup to an ovenproof dish and add the rhubarb, Grenadine and ginger. Cook in the oven for 10–15 minutes or until the rhubarb just gives but holds its shape. Drain off the juice into a small saucepan and mix a little of the juice with the cornflour to form a paste. Add this to the rest of the juice and cook until the mixture thickens.

7 To make the rhubarb cloud, soak the gelatine in cold water for about 5 minutes to soften and then squeeze to drain. Heat the sugar with 45ml of water in a saucepan until dissolved, then add the gelatine to the warm sugar liquid. Put 100ml of the thickened rhubarb sauce into the

bowl of an electric mixer with the balloon whisk attachment and, mixing on slow speed, add the sugar mix. Increase the speed to full until the mix foams up and forms firm peaks. Spoon into a square dish and leave it to set in the fridge for at least 1 hour before cutting it into squares.

8 For the caramelised cream, soak the gelatine in cold water for about 5 minutes to soften and then squeeze to drain. Combine the milk and cream in a saucepan and bring to the boil. Split the vanilla pod in half lengthways and scrape out the seeds. Put the seeds and pod into the cream mixture, remove from the heat and allow to infuse. While still warm, add the gelatine to the vanilla cream.

9 Meanwhile, put the egg yolks and sugar into a bowl set over a saucepan of barely simmering water and whisk for about 10 minutes or until the yolks have thickened. Continuing to whisk, strain the vanilla cream onto the eggs and then mix in the agar agar.

10 Transfer the vanilla cream to a clean pan and, continuously stirring, gently heat until it starts to thicken, but do not let it boil as this will scramble the eggs. To test the cream, dip a spoon into the mixture and run a finger through the cream on the back. If it leaves a line, it is ready. Pour into a shallow container measuring approximately 15 x 11cm, so the cream is about 1cm thick, and leave to set in the fridge.

11 Cut the cream into 1.5cm-wide strips and scatter with brown sugar. Then use a blow torch to caramelise the top. Please note that the cream must be not exposed to too much heat or it will melt before browning.

12 To serve, place some poached rhubarb pieces on each plate and scatter baked crumble pieces over the fruit. Add a strip of caramel cream, some cloud and a biscuit. Run lines of the thickened rhubarb sauce along the plates and then make quenelles of the sorbet, place onto a little cluster of crumble and decorate with coconut shards.

RUPERT ROWLEY
FISCHER'S BASLOW HALL

Since he took over the kitchen, Rupert Rowley has brought a touch of lightness and modernity to Baslow Hall. Max and Susan Fischer's stewardship of this romantic, ivy-clad manor house-with-rooms began in 1988, and a few years later the Sheffield-born Rowley, then a 16-year-old catering student, did his first stint in the hotel's kitchen. Subsequently, Rowley worked for Raymond Blanc, John Burton Race and Gordon Ramsay before his return to Baslow Hall as head chef seven years ago. As well as incorporating excellent Derbyshire ingredients, his outward-looking modern European menu employs what *The Good Food Guide 2010* calls 'stunning technique, invention and deep, intense flavours'.

Rowley is a huge fan of Baslow Hall's quirky charms, born of long-term independent ownership, and so are many of *The Good Food Guide*'s readers and inspectors; it's one of the most popular restaurants on the Guide's Top 50 list. The Fischers remain a presence and, along with their head chef, they also own Rowley's, a brasserie down the road with a more relaxed, hearty take on local produce – including the famous Henderson's relish, the 'spicy Yorkshire sauce' made in Sheffield. Meanwhile, back at Fischer's, Rowley can be found constructing his toasted marshmallow dessert with passion fruit sorbet and mango (see overleaf).

'The country house hotel is something unique to England and should be kept alive, especially the independently owned ones. A lot of blood, sweat and tears has made Fischer's what it is.'

Fischer's Baslow Hall | Calver Road, Baslow, Derbyshire DE45 1RR
(01246) 583259 | **www.fischers-baslowhall.co.uk**

KITCHEN
GARDEN

Toasted marshmallow with passion fruit sorbet and mango
Rupert Rowley

SERVES 4–6

FOR THE TOASTED MARSHMALLOW
4g gelatine leaves
160g caster sugar
30g glucose
2 egg whites

FOR THE STOCK SYRUP
700g caster sugar

FOR THE PASSION FRUIT JELLY
3g gelatine leaves
75ml passion fruit juice
25ml orange juice

FOR THE PASSION FRUIT SORBET
250ml passion fruit juice
25g sorbet stabiliser (optional)

FOR THE PISTACHIO SOIL
40g pistachios, ground to a powder
25g ground almonds
50g caster sugar
60g plain flour
Pinch of salt
40g butter, melted

FOR THE LIME TUILES
50g isomalt
Grated zest of ½ lime
25g pistachios, chopped

FOR THE MANGO
Grated zest of 1 lime
1 mango, peeled, stoned and chopped

TO SERVE
2–3 sprigs of coriander (micro if available)

Specific equipment: see page 259

1 To make the marshmallow, soak the gelatine in cold water for about 5 minutes to soften and then squeeze to drain. Meanwhile, put the sugar, glucose and 50ml of water into a saucepan and gently bring to the boil. Put the egg whites in a food processor and whisk them to soft peaks. When the syrup reaches 140°C, add the gelatine. Then pour the syrup over the whipped egg whites and whisk until the mixture has reached room temperature.

2 Scrape the mix onto a silicone sheet, place another sheet over the top and press to about 2cm thick. Put into the fridge to set. When firm, peel off the silicone and cut the marshmallow into four or six 4 x 10cm rectangles. Set aside.

3 To make the stock syrup, put 700ml of water into a pan, add the sugar and bring to the boil. Remove from the heat and leave to cool.

4 For the passion fruit jelly, soak the gelatine in cold water for about 5 minutes to soften and then squeeze to drain. Put the fruit juices in a saucepan together with 60ml of the stock syrup and bring to the boil. Add the gelatine to the juice and stir until dissolved. Pour into a 15 x 20cm shallow container and chill to set. Cut into 2cm cubes.

5 For the passion fruit sorbet, put the passion fruit juice into a bowl and add 125ml of water, 300ml of the stock syrup and the sorbet stabiliser, if using. Mix well and then freeze in an ice-cream machine according to the manufacturer's instructions.

6 To make the pistachio soil, preheat the oven to 180°C/Gas 4. Put the ground pistachios and almonds into an ovenproof dish, together with the sugar, flour and salt, and mix together. Pour the butter over the mixture, mix again and then bake for 30 minutes or until golden. Allow to cool and then crumble with your hands.

7 For the lime tuiles, gently melt the isomalt in a saucepan and add the lime zest and pistachios. Pour onto a silicone sheet and leave to cool. When cool enough to touch, tear off shards to decorate the dish.

8 To prepare the mango, bring 100ml of the stock syrup to the boil in a saucepan and add the lime zest and mango pieces. Take the pan off the heat and allow to cool.

9 To assemble, place a marshmallow rectangle in the centre of each plate and toast lightly with a blow torch. Add a few cubes of jelly and sprinkle with the soil. Drain the mango and arrange 3 pieces on each plate. Finally, place a quenelle of the passion fruit sorbet at one end of the marshmallow, add some lime tuiles and decorate the plates with the coriander. Serve immediately.

'The flavour of toasted marshmallow can bring a lot of childhood memories back. It's a fun dish, and eating the trimmings is a bonus.'

GLYNN PURNELL
PURNELL'S

One of the new generation of exciting British chefs, and with the trademark non-traditional whites to prove it, Glynn Purnell is still fanatical about working every service at his eponymous Birmingham restaurant. After starting in kitchens at 14 years of age, he came here from the relatively local, but decidedly less urban, high-fliers Simpsons, Jessica's and the Ludlow incarnation of Hibiscus. By contrast, Purnell's, with its thrusting brick-and-metal interior and prints of Brummie scenes, may seem harsh. It's tempered, however, by Purnell's notorious sense of humour, which is evident in his food as well as audible through the kitchen walls as service eases up.

His egg surprise with marinated strawberries, served next to a vanilla English custard-filled eggshell with a light strawberry sorbet (see overleaf), is unlikely to leave the menu after it came into the public eye on *Great British Menu*. It demonstrates the witty sideways thinking that's also evident in Purnell's (Abigail's) party piece of goat's cheese royale and pineapple on sticks. Elsewhere, Purnell feeds the multicultural flavours of Birmingham through a dish of coconut-poached brill with expertly spiced lentils. These little jokes are not done at the expense of flavour or good looks, however; the food here may raise a smile and perhaps an eyebrow, but it's carefully thought out and meticulously presented.

'The problem I've got with being in a city centre is that people do crave a bit for the countryside. It's nice to bring it into the restaurant.'

Purnell's | 55 Cornwall Street, Birmingham B3 2DH
(0121) 212 9799 | **www.purnellsrestaurant.com**

Egg surprise with marinated strawberries, strawberry sorbet and black pepper honeycomb

Glynn Purnell

**MAKES 4 INDIVIDUAL
EGG SURPRISES**

FOR THE HONEYCOMB

100g caster sugar

20g clear honey

35ml liquid glucose

5g bicarbonate of soda

Freshly ground black pepper

**FOR THE MARINATED
STRAWBERRIES**

100g caster sugar

100ml Banyuls sweet red wine

2 star anise

6–7 strawberries per person,
cut in half if large

FOR THE CARAMEL

70g caster sugar

**FOR THE ENGLISH
CUSTARD**

4 eggs

30g caster sugar, plus extra
for sprinkling

170ml double cream

1 vanilla pod, split in half
lengthways

TO SERVE

Strawberry sorbet

Small bunch of tarragon,
deep-fried in vegetable oil
until crisp

**Specific equipment:
see page 259**

1 To make the honeycomb, place the sugar, honey, glucose and 1 tbsp of water into a saucepan (this amount will double in volume so make sure you have a big enough pan) and boil until the liquid reaches 150°C on a thermometer. Add the bicarbonate of soda and quickly whisk to combine. The mixture will rise up in the pan when the bicarbonate of soda is added, so be careful. Immediately pour the mixture into a non-stick baking tray. Add several grindings of black pepper and set aside to cool, uncovered. Break into shards.

2 For the marinated strawberries, place the sugar, red wine, 35ml of water and star anise into a saucepan and simmer over a low heat until the liquid has reduced by half. Pour it over the strawberries in a small bowl and leave to infuse for 30 minutes.

3 To make the caramel, grease a non-stick baking sheet. Put the sugar and 2 tbsp of water into a shallow saucepan and boil until the sugar turns golden-brown. Brush the side of the pan with extra water every 40 seconds. Pour onto the baking sheet and leave to cool. When the caramel has set, shatter into shards.

4 For the burnt English custard, remove the tops of the eggs with a special egg-top remover, or carefully use a very sharp serrated knife, and separate the yolks from the whites. Set aside 1 of the yolks and the egg whites for another recipe (such as meringue; they will keep covered in the fridge for 2 days) and place the remaining 3 egg yolks in a bowl. Remove the membrane and clean and dry the egg shells.

5 Add the sugar to the egg yolks and whisk together until pale and fluffy. Pour the cream into a small pan, add the vanilla pod and place over a gentle heat to infuse the custard with the vanilla. When it is just below boiling point, remove from the heat, discard the vanilla pod and pour the hot custard over the egg yolks and sugar and whisk until combined. Pour the mixture into a clean pan, return to a gentle heat and stir until the mix starts to thicken enough to coat the back of a wooden spoon. Set aside and leave to cool slightly.

6 Carefully spoon the custard into the cleaned egg shells and set aside in an empty egg box to keep them level.

7 To serve, sprinkle a little caster sugar over the custard in each egg and caramelise using a blow torch. Serve the egg in a small eggcup on a plate with a quenelle of strawberry sorbet and the infused strawberries alongside decorated with black pepper honeycomb and caramel and scattered with deep-fried tarragon leaves.

'Black pepper brings out the natural sweetness of strawberries and tarragon enhances the flavour too. The honeycomb is a sweet texture that gives it a bit of a crunch. The eggshell's crunchy as well – but don't eat that!'

GUY MANNING
RED LION

It says something for the reorientation of British cooking in modern times that a destination address might as easily be found in a rural backwater – in this case on a bend in a Wiltshire B-road on the fringes of Salisbury Plain – as amid the bright lights of the city. Here, one of a new generation of young British chefs, Guy Manning, has made his home, after the kind of early experience that gets you noticed.

Following an in-at-the-deep-end, three-year apprenticeship at Bruce Poole's Chez Bruce in Wandsworth, a break was in order. On holiday in New York, Manning put his head round the door of the kitchens at high-end eatery Per Se and asked if there were any jobs going. 'Go home and call me when you're sober,' its then head chef Jonathan Benno coolly replied. Manning did just that, and soon progressed from a *stage* at Per Se to Martin Berasategui's award-laden restaurant in the Basque country.

From New York via San Sebastian to East Chisenbury is a very 21st-century kind of trajectory, but here in this modest-looking country pub, Manning is aiming high and in *The Good Food Guide 2010* garnered the Editors' Award for Best Pub Chef. Assiduously cultivating local suppliers, he builds his menus around fine produce in a style of cooking – deep-fried whitebait, roast Middle White pork loin with spectacular wands of crackling like grissini – that feels domestically familiar, but astonishes diners with its intensity. 'Gastropub' is quite the wrong label. This food looks restaurant-smart, yet is presented without overbearing reverence.

> *'I always had an ambition to be a pub chef, working with that style of food and doing the very best you can.'*

Red Lion | East Chisenbury, Wiltshire SN9 6AQ
(01980) 671124 | **www.redlionfreehouse.com**

Baked Alaska with passion fruit sorbet
Guy Manning

MAKES 4 INDIVIDUAL ALASKAS

200g passion fruit sorbet

FOR THE GINGER SPONGE

90g plain flour
¾ tsp baking powder
1 tsp ground ginger
Pinch of salt
2 eggs
90g light soft brown sugar
55g glucose
40g butter
2 tbsp milk

FOR THE MACADAMIA CRUNCH

75g macadamia nuts
25g glucose
50g caster sugar

FOR THE COULIS

3 passion fruit
20g caster sugar

FOR THE ROOT GINGER TUILES

10cm fresh root ginger, skin left on
200g caster sugar
1 tbsp demerara sugar

FOR THE MERINGUE

2 egg whites
120g caster sugar

Specific equipment: see page 259

1 To make the ginger sponge, preheat the oven to 170°C/Gas 3. Line a 23cm-diameter cake tin with baking parchment and grease well. Sift the flour, baking powder, ground ginger and salt into a bowl. Put the eggs and brown sugar into an electric-mixer bowl fitted with a whisk attachment (or use a hand-held electric mixer). Beat on high speed for about 5 minutes or until very light in colour, stiff and airy. Lightly fold in the dry ingredients.

2 Slowly melt the glucose and butter in a small saucepan or microwave until very hot, but do not allow to boil. Fold the milk into the sponge mix. Then gently fold in the hot glucose and butter until it has been absorbed. Pour into the cake tin and bake for 18–20 minutes or until just firm to the touch or a skewer inserted in the middle comes out clean. Leave in the tin to cool (but keep the oven turned on), then refrigerate in the tin for about 1 hour.

3 To make the macadamia crunch, put the nuts on a baking sheet and bake in the oven for about 10 minutes or until toasted. Put the glucose and caster sugar in a pan. Cook over a medium heat for about 10 minutes or until it begins to caramelise. Remove from the heat and add the nuts. Pour onto baking parchment and leave to cool, then finely chop.

4 To start assembling the Alaskas, remove the sponge from the tin, trim to create a flat, even layer of cake and then cut it into four 7cm-diameter discs and place on a baking tray. Using an ice-cream scoop, take a portion of sorbet, scrape the bottom flush with the edge of the scoop and turn onto a sponge disc. Repeat with the remaining discs. Gently press a thin layer of the macadamia crunch all over each scoop, reserving the rest to decorate. Place in the freezer and leave for at least 1 hour.

5 To make the coulis, chop and deseed the passion fruit. Put the flesh in a pan with the sugar and reserve the seeds. Bring to the boil, reduce the heat and simmer for 5 minutes to allow it to reduce by about a quarter. Leave to cool.

6 To make the tuiles, preheat the oven to 100°C/Gas ¼. Use a mandoline or very sharp knife to slice the ginger lengthways into wafer-thin pieces. Put the caster sugar in a pan with 100ml of water and bring to the boil to make a syrup. Add the ginger slices and boil for 10 minutes. Remove the slices from the pan and lay carefully on a baking tray, well covered with the syrup. Sprinkle with demerara sugar and then bake in the oven for 1 hour or until dry.

7 Up to an hour before serving, make the meringue. Place the egg whites and sugar in a bowl and stir over a saucepan of simmering water until the sugar has dissolved and the mixture is warm. Whisk in an electric mixer or with a hand-held mixer until the meringue forms stiff peaks. Place in a piping bag with a straight tip and pipe it around and over each sorbet scoop. With a butter knife, lift parts of the meringue to create spikes. Return to the freezer for at least 30 minutes.

8 When ready to serve, preheat the oven to 200°C/Gas 6. When the oven is hot, transfer the Alaskas from the freezer to the oven for about 3 minutes or until the meringue is just beginning to brown. Transfer the Alaskas to plates. Decorate with the passion fruit coulis with some of the seeds added, the leftover macadamia crunch and the ginger tuiles. Serve immediately.

MATTHEW TOMKINSON
MONTAGU ARMS HOTEL, TERRACE RESTAURANT

Although Matthew Tomkinson initially took a degree in hotel management, he had always wanted to become a chef because he thought it sounded 'ridiculously glamorous'. At first attracted more by the camaraderie, the macho swagger of working in a kitchen, than the food, the chance acquisition of a copy of Nico Ladenis's book *My Gastronomy* opened his eyes. Then along came *White Heat.*

The imagery in Marco Pierre White's groundbreaking book turned Tomkinson's life around – 'this was how food should be, this was something I could do for the rest of my life' – and he set out to make it happen. His big break came in 2005 when he won the Roux scholarship and a three-month stint at Michel Guérard's Les Prés d'Eugénie.

'Get the hospitality right and make people feel welcome – there's something very special about that.'

Now settled in as head chef at the Montagu Arms, Tomkinson is a culinary star in the making. This may be a traditionally appointed country house hotel but Tomkinson's kitchen takes a clean, modern approach. The abundance of stunning produce from the New Forest and the nearby coast is the inspiration; fresh, seasonal ingredients shape the cooking, and the flavours just shine.

Montagu Arms Hotel, Terrace Restaurant | Palace Lane, Beaulieu, Hampshire SO42 7ZL
(01590) 612324 | **www.montaguarmshotel.co.uk**

Warm pistachio sponge cake with rhubarb sorbet, rhubarb compote and vanilla custard

Matthew Tomkinson

SERVES 6–8

FOR THE PURÉE
700g rhubarb
2 tsp caster sugar

FOR THE RHUBARB CRISP
10g icing sugar

FOR THE SORBET
200g caster sugar
1 tbsp liquid glucose
Juice of 2 lemons

FOR THE COMPOTE
50g caster sugar
100g rhubarb
50ml Grenadine

FOR THE CUSTARD
200ml whole milk
200ml double cream
1 vanilla pod
25g custard powder
110g caster sugar
5 egg yolks

FOR THE SPONGE
1 egg and 2 egg yolks
75g caster sugar
65ml olive oil
50g pistachio paste (or ground unsalted pistachios)
50g butter, melted and cooled
25g polenta
25g plain flour
2 tsp baking powder
Grated zest and juice of ½ lemon
Grated zest of ½ orange

1 First make some rhubarb purée. Trim and chop the rhubarb and place in a saucepan together with a splash of water, then gently heat until the rhubarb is very soft. Transfer to a food processor and purée. Set aside 100g for the rhubarb crisp and 500g for the sorbet and then sweeten the remaining purée with the caster sugar. The finished purée should be tart so as to balance the dish, but if you prefer it a little sweeter, add some more sugar to taste. Store in the fridge.

2 For the rhubarb crisp, mix together the reserved 100g of rhubarb purée with the icing sugar until well combined and then spread very thinly on a non-stick baking sheet. Leave it to dry for 24–36 hours in an airing cupboard. When it is dry but still warm, break into pieces and store in an airtight container.

3 For the sorbet, add the sugar, glucose and lemon juice and 200ml of water to a saucepan. Bring to the boil, reduce the heat and simmer for 5 minutes. Allow the mixture to cool and combine with the reserved 500g of rhubarb purée. Pass through a fine sieve and freeze in an ice-cream machine according to the manufacturer's instructions.

4 For the compote, put the sugar in a saucepan with 120ml of water and bring to the boil to make a light syrup. Leave to cool. Cut the rhubarb into batons 1cm thick and 4cm long and place in the syrup along with the Grenadine. Return the pan to the heat and bring up to 65°C. Remove from the heat, cover the pan with a lid, leave for 15 minutes and then transfer to the fridge to chill. Dice into 1cm cubes and mix with a little of the sweetened purée to form a compote.

5 To make the custard, put the milk, cream and vanilla pod in a saucepan and bring to the boil. In a separate bowl, beat together the custard powder, sugar and egg yolks until pale and creamy. Strain the milk mixture over the custard, whisking all the time, then return this mix to the pan and cook gently until it reaches 75°C. Pour back into the bowl, place over ice to cool rapidly and then put in the fridge to chill.

6 For the sponge, preheat the oven to 160°C/Gas 3 and line a 23 x 18 x 4cm baking tray with greaseproof paper. Using a hand-held electric mixer, beat the eggs and the sugar together in a bowl until pale and creamy, then slowly add the olive oil, pistachio paste (or ground nuts) and the butter, continuing to beat. Gently fold in the rest of the ingredients and pour into the baking tray. Cook for 20–30 minutes or until risen and golden.

7 To serve, put small spoonfuls of the sweetened purée randomly across the centre of each plate and place wedges of the warm sponge cake over them. Add scoops of the sorbet and custard and then intersperse with spoonfuls of the rhubarb compote. Insert pieces of the rhubarb crisp into the sorbet and serve immediately.

'It's quite a traditional dessert – sponge cake paired with rhubarb and custard; it's tangy, it's soothing, it's warm and looks good on the plate.'

JAMES GRAHAM
ALLIUM

There can't be many chefs with a masters degree in diplomatic theory, but it was while studying at Leicester University that James Graham got a job in a local restaurant simply because 'I had to work to live'. Luckily for the food world, Graham soon realised that diplomacy wasn't for him. So began a career as a chef and restaurateur that was first recognised by *The Good Food Guide* when Graham ran the restaurant at Wickham Vineyard.

With the help of his wife Erica, Graham has continued to score highly in *The Good Food Guide*, and the couple replicated their earlier success when they opened Allium in 2004 in a pair of centuries-old stone houses on the market square in Fairford in the Cotswolds.

Allium's dishes display a vivid sense of seasonality and the precise cooking combines great technical aplomb with a degree of refinement – for example, 'low temperature' organic salmon is served with a frogs' leg Kiev, while wild sea bass is accompanied by spelt and wild mushrooms.

A keen forager and champion of wild food, Graham sources much of the produce he uses himself and employs the most up-to-date cooking techniques to 'bring out the true flavours of the best local ingredients'. His blood orange and beetroot dessert (see overleaf) is a fine example of his impeccably presented dishes, one that 'hints that spring will soon arrive, even when we serve it in January – it's fresh and deeply satisfying.'

'I'm inspired by chefs who have achieved consistency over long careers, and I still want to be better every day.'

Allium | 1 London Street, Fairford, Gloucestershire GL7 4AH
(01285) 712200 | **www.alliumfood.co.uk**

Blood orange delice with beetroot sorbet and chocolate powder
James Graham

SERVES 8

FOR THE BEETROOT SORBET
500g beetroot juice
180g caster sugar
1 tbsp glucose syrup

FOR THE JOCONDE SPONGE
3 egg whites
15g caster sugar
2 large eggs
100g ground almonds, sifted
100g icing sugar, sifted
25g plain flour
20g butter, melted

FOR THE ITALIAN MERINGUE
45g caster sugar
1 egg white

FOR THE BLOOD ORANGE MOUSSE
5g gelatine leaves
250g blood orange purée, warmed
150g double cream, whipped

FOR THE BLOOD ORANGE JELLY
2g gelatine leaves
125ml blood orange juice

FOR THE CHOCOLATE POWDER
80g caster sugar
100ml still mineral water
40g dark chocolate (53% cocoa solids),
  melted

TO SERVE
1 blood orange, segmented
Crystallised orange peel (optional)

Specific equipment: see page 259

1 For the beetroot sorbet, place all the ingredients in a saucepan together with 320ml of water. Bring to the boil, then leave to cool and freeze in an ice-cream machine according to the manufacturer's instructions.

2 For the joconde sponge, preheat the oven to 200°C/Gas 6 and line a 23 x 18 x 4cm baking tray with greaseproof-paper. Put the egg whites and caster sugar in a bowl and whisk until fluffy. In another bowl, whisk together the eggs, almonds and icing sugar until the mixture has reached ribbon stage. Sift in the flour and fold in gently. Pour the melted butter into the mix and then fold in the beaten egg whites. Spread out on the tray in a 3mm-thick layer and bake for 10–15 minutes or until cooked evenly. Allow to cool.

3 To make the Italian meringue, put 1 tbsp of water and the sugar in a small saucepan and gently heat to a temperature of 118°C. Whisk the egg white in an electric mixer to soft peaks and then add the sugar syrup, continuing to whisk. Leave the mixer on a medium speed and continue to whisk until the meringue has cooled.

4 For the blood orange mousse, soak the gelatine in cold water for about 5 minutes to soften and then squeeze to drain. Add to the purée and mix. Fold in the Italian meringue and then the cream.

5 To start assembling the blood orange delice, use a metal frame measuring 10 x 10cm to cut out a square of the sponge (there will be more than you need – use the rest for a roulade). Then pour the mousse over the sponge, leaving 1mm space at the top in the frame. Allow to set in the fridge while you make the jelly.

6 To make the blood orange jelly, soak the gelatine in cold water for about 5 minutes to soften and then squeeze to drain. Warm the juice and add the gelatine. Leave to cool to room temperature. Take the delice from the fridge and top with a shallow layer of jelly. Return to the fridge to set.

7 To make the chocolate powder, put the sugar and water into a saucepan and gently heat to 150°C. Remove from the heat and pour in the melted chocolate. Stir vigorously with a fork for about 1 minute or until the chocolate has crystallised.

8 To serve, crumble some of the chocolate powder across each plate and arrange a few blood orange segments to one side. Cut the delice into 8 slices and position a slice on the other side of the plate. Then top the orange segments with a scoop of the beetroot sorbet decorated with crystallised orange peel, if using.

'Beetroot and blood orange are in season at the same time; the subtle citrus bitterness of the orange balances beautifully with the earthy sweetness of the beetroot.'

SHAUN HILL
THE WALNUT TREE

It was an interest in eating, rather than cooking, that first prompted Shaun Hill to become a chef. Having left school with A levels in Latin, Greek and ancient history, Hill was all set for a more academic path, but he turned down a place at university and, in 1966, went to work at Robert Carrier's eponymous restaurant in Camden Passage in north London.

After working his way through a number of notable kitchens, including The Gay Hussar and The Capital, he left London in the early 1980s and opened Hill's in Stratford-upon-Avon, which is when he first came to the notice of *The Good Food Guide*, before moving to other illustrious venues (see right).

Hill became joint owner of The Walnut Tree in 2008 and has successfully recreated its stellar reputation following the closure of the restaurant after its long-standing owners Franco and Ann Taruschio retired from the business. Hill makes the food look deceptively simple and uses only the best ingredients available to him. He uses local produce, but only when it's good, noting that 'you wouldn't eat in a rubbish restaurant just because it was a 100 yards closer than a good one.'

The road to The Walnut Tree
Hill has rarely been out of *The Good Food Guide* since he opened Hill's in Stratford-upon-Avon, high-scoring at Gidleigh Park, the Merchant House in Ludlow and now The Walnut Tree in Abergavenny. He still cooks most days, despite being only two years away from retirement age, because, 'I rather like cooking but not meetings and bureaucracy.'

The Walnut Tree | Llanddewi Skirrid, Gwent NP7 8AW
(01873) 852797 | **www.thewalnuttreeinn.com**

'As I have become older I am more inclined to look back wistfully at the past glories of cooking and less inclined to get excited over the latest bit of foam or rectangular crockery.'

Buttermilk pudding with baked cardamom figs

Shaun Hill

MAKES 4 INDIVIDUAL PUDDINGS

FOR THE PUDDINGS

1½ gelatine leaves
200ml double cream
125g caster sugar
½ vanilla pod, split in half lengthways
2 strips orange peel
1 tbsp lemon juice
300ml buttermilk

FOR THE FIGS

6 figs, cut in half
1 tsp crushed cardamom seeds
1 tbsp caster sugar
Juice of ½ orange
1 tbsp clear honey

Specific equipment: see page 259

1 To make the pudding, soak the gelatine in cold water for about 5 minutes to soften and then squeeze to drain. Meanwhile, put 100ml of the double cream with the sugar, vanilla pod and orange peel into a saucepan and bring to the boil. Remove from the heat and add the lemon juice and gelatine. Mix and strain into a clean jug.

2 Put the buttermilk in a bowl, then gradually whisk in the strained hot cream. Let the mixture cool. Whip the remaining double cream and fold into the buttermilk. Spoon the mix into four 125ml crème caramel or dariole moulds or ramekins and refrigerate overnight.

3 Preheat the oven to 200°C/Gas 6. Arrange the figs in an ovenproof baking dish, sprinkle over the cardamom, sugar and orange juice and pour the honey over the figs. Bake for about 10 minutes or until hot, then remove from the oven.

4 To serve, turn each pudding out onto a serving plate. Place 3 fig halves around each pudding together with a little of their cooking liquor.

'I like this buttermilk pudding dish because it's so easy and not too sweet and gooey. At the end of a meal, I want my palate freshened, rather than flattened by lots of sugar.'

SKYE GYNGELL
PETERSHAM NURSERIES CAFÉ

The once-mandatory practice of eating only what was available when it became available has had a major resurgence in the 21st century. It may require a leap of faith to understand the rhythms of the seasons at a restaurant in the big city, but stray a little way off the urban path, even just as far as Richmond Park and the banks of the Thames, and it all starts making sense.

When friends who had bought a garden centre showed Skye Gyngell the place, she 'completely fell in love with it', instantly seeing its potential as a dining venue. What was once a restaurant in a potting shed with a blackboard menu of three dishes a day has now become a little more expansive in its ambitions. Despite this, you still eat amid the ambience of an English garden, either outdoors or among the greenhouse plants, as you wish.

It's a daytime venue of singular charm, where even the shortest seasons of domestic produce – the six weeks of asparagus, the damson's mere three – are accorded due prominence. The culinary approach may embrace some of the best Italian, French, even Middle Eastern styles, but at its heart is the excitement that comes from a climate that can change from week to week, bestowing its bounty as it goes.

'Seasonality is so important. If you just choose to work with that, the culinary possibilities unfold before your eyes.'

Petersham Nurseries Café | Church Lane, off Petersham Road, Richmond, London TW10 7AG
(020) 8605 3627 | **www.petershamnurseries.com**

Zuppa Inglese
Skye Gyngell

SERVES 4–6

300ml whole milk
Grated zest of 1 orange
Grated zest of ½ lemon
½ vanilla pod, split in half
   lengthways
4 eggs
60g caster sugar
30g plain flour, sifted
2½ tbsp cocoa powder
40g dark chocolate
   (70% cocoa solids), chopped
40ml limoncello
10–15 savoiardi biscuits (or
   sponge fingers)

**FOR THE CANDIED
ORANGE**

1 orange, peeled
125g caster sugar

1 To prepare the candied orange, slice the orange into fine rounds and blanch in a saucepan of boiling water for a minute or so. Drain and refresh in cold water. Repeat this process a further 2 times. Dissolve the sugar in 125ml of water in a small heavy-based pan over a medium heat then bring to the boil. Add the orange slices, reduce the heat slightly and cook for 10–15 minutes or until the syrup is viscous. Take off the heat and set aside to cool.

2 Pour the milk into a heavy-based pan and add the orange and lemon zest. Scrape the seeds from the vanilla pod and add to the pan together with the empty pod. Heat to a simmer, then remove from the heat and set aside to infuse for 15 minutes.

3 Whisk the eggs, sugar and flour with a hand-held electric mixer in a large bowl until the mixture is pale and thick. Slowly pour in the milk mixture, whisking as you do so. Pour back into the pan and continue to whisk over a low heat until the custard thickens enough to coat the back of a wooden spoon and no longer tastes floury. Immediately pour into two bowls, dividing equally, and discarding the vanilla pod. Add the cocoa powder and chocolate to one bowl and stir until the powder is evenly distributed and the chocolate has melted. Set the bowls of vanilla and chocolate custards aside to cool.

4 Drain the orange slices, reserving the syrup, and chop into small pieces. Then stir the limoncello into the syrup. Take 1 tbsp of the syrup and stir it into the vanilla custard. Split the savoiardi in half lengthways and sprinkle with the remaining syrup. Arrange a layer of the soaked savoiardi over the bottom of a serving bowl. Top with a layer of vanilla custard, then a scattering of chopped orange. Add another layer of savoiardi, followed by chocolate custard, then orange.

5 Continue in this way until you've used all the ingredients, finishing with a few spoonfuls each of the vanilla and chocolate custards. Swirl together to create a marbled effect, then refrigerate for at least 1 hour before serving. Alternatively, divide the ingredients between 4–6 bowls and serve as individual portions.

'I love the slightly old-fashioned air of this dish. It's unashamedly rich but charming, and you can just serve it out from the dish with a big old spoon.'

'As you gain more experience, you start to become more aware of creating menus that are well balanced, imaginative and taste great.'

MARTIN BURGE
WHATLEY MANOR

Although it was his mother's home cooking that first encouraged him to cook, it was a work experience placement at a Bristol catering college that inspired Martin Burge to become a professional chef. Since then, he has risen through the ranks of some of Britain's most respected kitchens, including Pied à Terre, L'Ortolan and Le Manoir aux Quat'Saisons. His early influences include Raymond Blanc 'for his energy and passion for great food', and John Burton Race (at The Landmark), 'who empowered me to express my style of food alongside his'. Burge left London in 2003 to take on the role of head chef at the sumptuous Wiltshire hotel and spa, Whatley Manor.

This is a chef who likes to keep diners on their toes with dishes that show a high level of complexity and superb presentation – langoustine tails are served with bacon glazed in soy and cauliflower purée and topped with Thai foam; squab pigeon arrives with coffee and sherry gel, roasted foie gras and baby turnips. Dishes are elaborately worked yet emerge from the kitchen with a deceptive air of effortlessness about them. Burge says his approach to food has developed over the years, partly because of the constantly evolving cooking techniques and new equipment, which 'enable chefs to express their passion for good food and realise their creativity in the menus'. His philosophy is to create a memorable dining experience and ensure that guests are happy and return.

Whatley Manor | Easton Grey, Wiltshire SN16 0RB
(01666) 822888 | **www.whatleymanor.com**

Chicory mousse layered with bitter coffee and mascarpone cream
Martin Burge

MAKES 4 INDIVIDUAL MOUSSES

FOR THE CHICORY MOUSSE
37g chicory beans
75ml full-fat milk, plus extra
185ml whipping cream
2 egg yolks
20g caster sugar
15g milk chocolate, melted
2.5g gelatine leaves

FOR THE COFFEE SYRUP
20g caster sugar
75g hot espresso coffee
50g Kahlua
50g Pedro Ximénez sherry

FOR THE JOCONDE SPONGE
95g icing sugar
95g ground almonds
3 large eggs, lightly beaten
20g unsalted butter, melted
15g caster sugar
3 egg whites
25g plain flour, sifted
15g dark chocolate (70% cocoa solids), melted

FOR THE MASCARPONE CREAM
55g caster sugar
2 egg yolks
85g mascarpone cheese
2g gelatine leaves
80ml whipping cream

FOR THE CHOCOLATE COATING
300g cocoa butter
300g dark chocolate (70% cocoa solids)

TO DECORATE
24 tempered chocolate leaves (4 x 3cm)
4 pieces of edible gold leaf (optional)
5g edible gold dust (optional)

Specific equipment: see page 259

1 To make the chicory mousse, toast the beans in a frying pan on a medium heat. Pour the milk and 75ml of the cream into a small saucepan, add the beans and leave to infuse for 30 minutes at a gentle heat, but check with a thermometer that the mixture does not exceed 70°C.
2 Weigh the infusion and add enough milk to make up to 125g. Whisk the egg yolks and sugar until pale and creamy. Meanwhile, bring the infusion to the boil, then pour it over the egg yolks and sugar. Return to the heat, stirring with a wooden spoon until the mixture has thickened to make a chicory crème anglaise. Pass through a fine sieve. Add the milk chocolate and set aside.
3 Soak the gelatine in cold water for about 5 minutes to soften and then squeeze to drain. Put 10ml of the remaining cream and all the gelatine in a pan and heat gently until it has dissolved. Remove from the heat, pour onto the chicory crème anglaise and whisk to mix. Whisk the remaining cream to form soft ribbons and fold into the chicory crème anglaise to finish the mousse. Pour the mixture into four 5cm-diameter half-sphere moulds and freeze.
4 For the coffee syrup, dissolve the sugar in the coffee. Add the Kahlua and sherry and set aside.
5 For the sponge, put the icing sugar, ground almonds and half the eggs into an electric mixer. Whisk on high for 8 minutes. Add the remainder of the eggs and whisk on high for 10 minutes more. Add the butter, whisk and set aside.
6 Preheat the oven to 220°C/Gas 6 and line a 23 x 18 x 4cm baking tray with greaseproof paper. Whisk the caster sugar and egg whites to soft peaks. Fold in the almond mixture and then the flour. With a palette knife, spread the mixture evenly over the tray. Bake for 10–12 minutes or until firm to the touch. Leave to cool and then spread a thin layer of the chocolate over the top. Using a 5cm-diameter hexagonal mould, cut out 8 hexagons. Set aside and discard any remaining sponge.
7 For the mascarpone cream, dissolve the sugar in 10ml of water in a pan and boil to 118°C to make a sugar syrup. Meanwhile, put the egg yolks in a mixing bowl, then pour in the sugar

syrup and whisk to form a sabayon. Set aside. In a separate bowl, whisk the mascarpone cheese until soft and smooth. Fold the sabayon into the mascarpone. Soften and drain the gelatine as in step 3. Put 5ml of the cream and all the gelatine in a pan and heat gently until it has dissolved. Remove from the heat, pour into the mascarpone mixture and whisk to combine. Whisk the remaining cream to form soft ribbons and fold into the mascarpone mixture.

8 Place a piece of sponge on the bottom of four 5cm-diameter hexagonal moulds, chocolate side down, and soak with 1 tbsp of the coffee syrup. Pipe in the mascarpone cream up to halfway. Repeat the layering of the sponge, syrup and the cream. Leave to set in the fridge for 2 hours.

9 For the chocolate coating, melt the cocoa butter and chocolate in a bain marie until it reaches 50–55°C, so the spray gun works well. Remove the chicory mousses from the freezer and turn out of their moulds by dipping them into cold water. Brush the bottom of each mousse with some of the melted chocolate in the bain marie, place on a baking tray, base side up, and return to the freezer for 10 minutes.

10 Pass the hot chocolate through a chinois or fine sieve into the spray gun. Line a baking tray with silicone paper. Remove the mousses from the freezer, lay, base side down, on the silicone paper, and quickly spray all over except the base. Place in the fridge to defrost.

11 Light the blow torch and heat the outside of each hexagonal mould to help remove the mousse from the mould. Place a chocolate-covered chicory mousse carefully on top of each mascarpone cream and then arrange the tempered chocolate leaves around the edge to form a hexagon. If using the gold leaf and gold dust, place pieces of gold leaf on top of each dome and lightly sprinkle the edge of the plate with gold dust.

'I love to revisit classic French dishes, seeking out the perfect foie gras, the perfect brioche.'

CLAUDE BOSI
HIBISCUS

Since leaving his native France in 1997 at the age of 22, Claude Bosi, the son of Lyonnaise bistro owners, has firmly made his mark on the UK restaurant scene – not bad for a young Frenchman who intended to stay for just six months to improve his English. His reputation was further enhanced in late 2007 when he forsook the small but glittering Ludlow constellation for the tooth-and-claw competitiveness of the London scene. After nine years in Ludlow this ambitious, idiosyncratic chef felt that he needed a new challenge.

Now in an intimate, panelled wood-and-slate dining room in Mayfair, Bosi is delivering some ingeniously inventive dishes. In essence, the cooking revisits his classic French training, but sideways thinking has always been a trademark and his food is as much about texture and flavour as respect for the past. Produce, too, is as pure as possible. For someone who admits to not having much of a sweet tooth, his desserts can be extraordinary, and the best remains the one described in *The Good Food Guide 2001*: 'the warm chocolate tart filled with black, sludgy, semi-runny chocolate is a hit' (see overleaf).

Hibiscus | 29 Maddox Street, Mayfair, London W1S 2PA
(020) 7629 2999 | **www.hibiscusrestaurant.co.uk**

Hibiscus tarte au chocolat
Claude Bosi

MAKES 8 INDIVIDUAL TARTES
FOR THE FILLING

100g dark chocolate (70% cocoa solids)
100g salted butter
3 eggs
100g caster sugar
45g plain flour

FOR THE PASTRY

150g unsalted butter, diced
75g caster sugar
100g cocoa powder
150g plain flour
1 egg
1 egg yolk

FOR THE SUGAR DECORATIONS

125g isomalt
25g glucose
½ star anise

TO SERVE

Cocoa powder for dusting
Ice cream

Specific equipment: see page 259

1 First make the filling. Put the chocolate and butter in a saucepan and gently melt. In a bowl, whisk together the eggs and sugar until light and fluffy and then whisk in the flour. Use a spatula to fold the melted chocolate and butter into the egg mixture.

2 Preheat the oven to 180°C/Gas 4 and grease eight 10cm-diameter, loose-bottomed cake tins.

3 For the pastry, cream the butter and sugar together in a bowl until pale and fluffy using a hand-held electric mixer. Sift in the cocoa powder and flour and mix, and then add the egg and egg yolk and blend together.

4 Divide the pastry into eight. On a lightly floured surface, roll out each piece and transfer to a prepared cake tin. Line the pastry cases with baking parchment and fill with dried beans or baking beans. Bake blind in the oven for 7 minutes. Remove the baking parchment and beans and allow the cases to cool.

5 Fill the cases with the filling mixture and return to the oven for about 10 minutes. Do not overcook – they should have the consistency of a brownie.

6 To make the sugar decorations, heat the isomalt and glucose in a saucepan until they reach 160°C. Pour out onto a baking sheet lined with silicone paper and leave for 5–10 minutes to cool.

7 Break the cooled mixture into small pieces and then blitz in a blender with the star anise to a fine powder. Sift the sugar carefully back onto the silicone paper so that the powder forms interesting flat shapes.

8 Heat the grill to hot and place the baking sheet under the grill for up to 2 minutes to allow the sugar to melt again. Leave to cool, carefully remove from the sheet and store in an airtight container until needed.

9 To serve the tartes au chocolat, dust each of them with cocoa powder while still warm and top with a scoop of ice cream and a sugar decoration.

'The tarte au chocolat is a fantastic, warm and runny pudding. I like to serve it with a Thai basil ice cream, which perfectly balances the richness of the chocolate.'

SAT BAINS
RESTAURANT SAT BAINS

Although he says he decided to become a chef because 'it was the queue with the most girls on when I went to an open day at college', Sat Bains has enjoyed a hugely successful career since winning the prestigious Roux scholarship at the first attempt in 1999. Today, he is a highly respected figure on the UK restaurant scene; his Nottingham restaurant is a destination address for diners from all over the UK and beyond.

The mantra 'location, location, location' may have passed him by when he committed to this restaurant-with-rooms at the end of a small lane next to a vast flyover, but the sensitively renovated Victorian farm buildings not far from the River Trent make an elegant if edgy setting for Bains' modern and complex cooking that has earned him the Editors' Award for Best Chef in *The Good Food Guide 2011*.

'I'm very fortunate not to have worked under any named chef, so a lot of what I've done has been self-explorative, allowing me to develop a unique outlook and vision to my food.'

Ingredients are so tersely enumerated on the trademark tasting menus they might be mistaken for shopping lists, but the pairing of unusual flavours and textures is clearly a passion. It's a very individual style in which the extraction of maximum flavour is seen by Bains as the most important element.

Restaurant Sat Bains | Lenton Lane, Nottingham NG7 2SA
(0115) 986 6566 | **www.restaurantsatbains.net**

Chocolate cream with rapeseed oil jelly, toast and sea salt

Sat Bains

SERVES 8

FOR THE CHOCOLATE TUILES

100g dark chocolate (70% cocoa solids)

2 egg whites

50g caster sugar

1 egg yolk

FOR THE CHOCOLATE CREAM

100ml milk

100ml cream

2 egg yolks

100g dark chocolate (70% cocoa solids)

FOR THE RAPESEED OIL JELLY

2g bronze gelatine leaves

15g caster sugar, plus extra for finishing

35g isomalt

90ml rapeseed oil

TO SERVE

Candied rose fragments

Candied violet fragments

Pinch of sea salt

Wafer-thin slices of sweet toast, baked until golden brown

1 To make the chocolate tuiles, preheat the oven to its lowest setting. Melt the chocolate in a bowl standing over a barely simmering saucepan of water. In a separate bowl, whip the egg whites and gradually add the sugar to make a meringue. Whisk the yolk into the chocolate, followed by the meringue, and then spread onto a baking sheet lined with silicone paper. Leave to dehydrate in the oven for 10–12 hours.

2 To make the chocolate cream, put the milk, cream and egg yolks into a saucepan and heat to 86°C, stirring carefully as the mixture thickens to prevent curdling. Put the chocolate in a heatproof bowl and pour the custard over the top, whisking until the chocolate is melted and you have a smooth cream. Leave to cool.

3 To make the rapeseed oil jelly, soak the gelatine in cold water for about 5 minutes to soften and then squeeze to drain. Put the caster sugar and isomalt into a saucepan, add 100ml of water and bring to the boil. Remove from the heat and whisk the gelatine into the syrup, then slowly whisk in the rapeseed oil. As the mixture cools, whisk every few moments to keep it emulsified. Pour into a bowl and leave in the fridge to set.

4 To serve, place a quenelle of the chocolate cream on each plate and top with the roses, violets and sea salt. Then add the pieces of toast and chocolate tuiles. To finish, cut the jelly into small pieces and roll in a little caster sugar before placing one piece of jelly next to each quenelle.

'The inspiration for this dish came from a trip to Spain where we watched families enjoy a snack based on chocolate, sea salt and olive oil. Here we use a locally produced virgin rapeseed oil, which has a lovely nutty flavour.'

ADAM SIMMONDS
DANESFIELD HOUSE

Identified in 2010 by *The Good Food Guide* as one of the ten chefs set to dominate the next decade, Adam Simmonds first knew he wanted to be a chef when he took a cookery class at school. 'I think I must have had a short attention span because standing by a stove with things changing minute by minute inspired me much more than answering maths questions at a desk,' he recalls.

Onwards and upwards

Adam Simmonds' rise to the top has been swift and, after three 'wonderful' years at Le Manoir aux Quat'Saisons, he came to the attention of *The Good Food Guide* when he was head chef at The Greenway in Gloucestershire. He went on to gain further recognition at Ynyshir Hall in Powys before taking over from Aiden Byrne at Danesfield House in February 2007.

Simmonds relishes taking the diner on a 'revelatory journey' in the panelled dining room of the Victorian Gothic hotel that is Danesfield House, but his creativity and modernity also comes with a sense of humour, such as with a lime and lager jelly with lime granita – a witty take on the drink. Flavours and textures are subtle, finely balanced and beautifully judged with dazzling combinations, such as langoustines teamed with yogurt, samphire, Oscietra caviar and cucumber essence. Simmonds says his style consists of classic roots combined with modern techniques, adding, 'I've learned to be more controlled in my cooking – although I am still a little fiery on the pass.'

Danesfield House | Henley Road, Marlow, Buckinghamshire SL7 2EY
(01628) 891010 | **www.danesfieldhouse.co.uk**

'I constantly assess myself and my methods and strive to be the best I can be.'

Chocolate, banana and rum millefeuille with banana parfait
Adam Simmonds

SERVES 4

FOR THE PRALINE TUILES
100g hazelnuts
150g caster sugar

FOR THE BANANA GANACHE
1.5g gelatine leaves
20ml milk
100g milk chocolate
100g banana purée
3g cocoa butter (if available)

FOR THE RUM JELLY
25g caster sugar
3g gelatine leaves
40ml dark rum

FOR THE MILK CHOCOLATE JELLY
3g gelatine leaves
50g milk chocolate (40% cocoa solids)

FOR THE HAZELNUT PURÉE
350ml milk
9g hazelnut oil
Small pinch of salt

FOR THE BANANA PARFAIT
2g gelatine leaves
3 large egg yolks
70g caster sugar
50g banana purée
150ml double cream, whipped

FOR THE BANANA MOUSSELINE
1.5g gelatine leaves
112g crème patissière
150g banana purée
25ml double cream, whipped

Specific equipment: see page 259

1 For the praline tuiles, preheat the oven to 180°C/Gas 4, roast the hazelnuts for 8–10 minutes, rub off their skins and roughly chop. Set half aside for the hazelnut purée. Dissolve the sugar in 3 tbsp of water, brushing the sides of the pan with water to ensure they stay clean and then increase the temperature and cook the liquid to a light caramel. Add the hazelnuts and stir to coat. Using a slotted spoon, transfer to a baking sheet lined with silicone paper and leave to cool. Then blitz in a blender to a powder. Set aside 25g for the ganache. Spread the rest thinly on a lined tray and bake for 5–7 minutes or until melted and golden. Leave to cool and break into pieces.

2 To make the banana ganache, soak the gelatine in cold water for about 5 minutes to soften and then squeeze to drain. In a small saucepan, heat the milk and the gelatine, mixing well. Melt the chocolate over a bain marie and warm to 45°C. Warm the banana purée in another saucepan, add to the milk and mix well and then add the reserved 25g of ground hazelnut caramel. Also melt the cocoa butter in a small dish in the microwave. Pour the banana purée slowly onto the chocolate, whisking with a hand-held electric mixer, and then, continuing to whisk, gradually pour in the cocoa butter. Cool then leave to rest in the fridge until set. Once set, pipe onto a lined baking sheet with a 2mm nozzle into three lines that are touching each other. Cut into eight 7.5 x 2.5cm rectangles.

3 For the rum jelly, line a flat-based container with cling film. Put the sugar and 100ml of water into a pan and bring to the boil. Leave to cool. Soak the gelatine in cold water for about 5 minutes to soften and squeeze to drain. Add to the syrup and then add the rum. Cool the liquor over ice until it thickens, then pour into the container and chill to set. Cut into 7.5 x 2.5cm rectangles.

4 For the milk chocolate jelly, line a 15 x 9cm shallow container with cling film. Soak the gelatine in cold water for about 5 minutes to soften and then squeeze to drain. Melt the chocolate over a bain marie and warm to 45°C. Put 100ml of water into a pan and heat to warm. Add the gelatine to the water, mixing well. Then pour onto the chocolate, while whisking with a hand-held electric mixer. Cool over ice, until it thickens, then pour into the container and chill to set. Cut into cubes.

> *'I enjoy putting together different flavours. Here, the chocolate and rum are perfectly complemented by the banana.'*

5 For the hazelnut purée, put the reserved chopped hazelnuts into a saucepan with the milk. Bring to the boil, then reduce the heat to a simmer and cook for about 25 minutes or until soft. Put the nuts and most of the milk into a blender and blitz to a purée, adding more of the milk if necessary. Pass through a fine sieve into a bowl and whisk in the hazelnut oil and salt. Taste and adjust if required.

6 For the banana parfait, line a 20 x 7cm shallow container with cling film. Soak the gelatine in cold water for about 5 minutes to soften and then squeeze to drain. Place the egg yolks in a food processor and start to whisk slowly. Put the sugar and 25ml of water in a pan and heat to 121°C. Pour the sugar over the egg yolks and continue to whisk. Add the gelatine and then turn the speed up to full and whisk until a cold, thick cream is achieved. Whisk in the banana purée and then fold in the cream. Pour into the container and place in the freezer to set.

7 For the banana mousseline, soak the gelatine in cold water for about 5 minutes to soften and then squeeze to drain. Whisk the crème patissière until smooth. Warm 50g of the banana purée in a pan and then add the gelatine. Mix well and leave to cool slightly. Add this to the crème patissière with the remaining purée and gelatine and mix well. Fold in the cream, transfer to a flat-based container and store in the fridge.

8 Spread the chocolate thinly onto sheets of acetate. Cut into sixteen 8 x 3cm rectangles and leave to cool and harden. For each millefeuille, layer the ingredients so you have a chocolate rectangle topped by banana ganache and rum jelly, three times, and finish with one more layer of chocolate (ten layers in total). Transfer to a plate and add dots of hazelnut purée, chocolate jelly cubes and small quenelles of the parfait. Insert shards of praline tuiles and cut out 2cm-diameter circles of the banana mousseline to finish.

ANTHONY FLINN
ANTHONY'S RESTAURANT

One of the best-known elBulli *stagiaires*, and one of the few eventually to make it onto the payroll, Anthony Flinn has been celebrated by *The Good Food Guide* since 2005. If it wasn't for the reputation for 'avant-garde excellence' acquired by the family Flinn (his father, sister and partner Olga are all very much involved in the business), one might walk straight past the unassuming but comfortable corner site at the station end of Leeds city centre. But downstairs, in a deliberately simple basement dining room, Flinn and his team are engaged in the kind of magical thinking that pairs the comforting flavours of, say, a classic risotto of white onion with a shock of espresso, or a damply aromatic banana cake with a jugful of pale but very interesting mozzarella velouté.

'If somebody says you can't do it, I go out of my way to do it. I don't know why, but I am what I am.'

The business has expanded apace since Flinn set out his bold and imaginative stall, and now, with a patisserie and the impressive Piazza by Anthony in the old Corn Exchange (also listed in the Guide), there is, it seems, an Anthony's for every occasion. Though the casual options can be a delight, it's the original, and most upmarket, restaurant that still seduces with its relaxed, urbane vibe. This is where Flinn's expertise is most gratifyingly displayed, and where a man of relatively few words speaks most eloquently through his food.

Anthony's Restaurant | 19 Boar Lane, Leeds LS1 6EA
(0113) 245 5922 | **www.anthonysrestaurant.co.uk**

Chocolate and peppermint cheesecake with vanilla salt caramel and caramelised hazelnuts

Anthony Flinn

SERVES 4

FOR THE CHEESECAKE
110ml double cream
175g mascarpone cheese
200g milk chocolate, melted
50g caster sugar
2 tsp peppermint extract

FOR THE VANILLA SALT CARAMEL
100g caster or granulated sugar
100ml double cream
200ml milk
Pinch of vanilla salt (or pinch of salt with 4 drops vanilla extract)
5g lecithin

FOR THE BRITTLE
25g butter
50g caster or granulated sugar
Pinch of salt

FOR THE CARAMELISED HAZELNUTS
100g hazelnuts
150g caster sugar

TO DECORATE
Natural yogurt
Mint leaves

Specific equipment:
see page 259

1 Cut 4 rectangles of acetate each measuring 10 x 25cm and roll into 25cm-long tubes with a diameter of about 2cm. Secure with sticky tape and put in the fridge to chill.

2 To make the cheesecake, put the cream and mascarpone into a saucepan and bring to the boil. Melt the chocolate over a bain marie and pour the cream mixture over the top. Add the caster sugar and peppermint flavouring and whisk until smooth. Pour into the acetate tubes and allow to set in the fridge or freezer.

3 To make the vanilla salt caramel, place the sugar and a splash of water in a saucepan, gently heat until the sugar dissolves then bring to the boil and cook for about 10 minutes or until golden brown. Do not let it start to burn. Once the sugar has caramelised, take it off the heat and then whisk in the cream and milk, a little at a time. Allow to cool then chill in the fridge and whisk in the salt and lecithin.

4 For the brittle, put the ingredients in a pan and boil together for about 10 minutes or until golden brown. Pour onto a non-stick baking sheet lined with silicone paper into a thin layer and leave to cool. Break into shards.

5 Caramelise the hazelnuts by dissolving the sugar in 3 tbsp of water, brushing the sides of the pan with water to ensure they stay clean, and then increase the temperature and cook the liquid to a light caramel. Add the hazelnuts and stir to coat. Using a slotted spoon, transfer to a baking sheet lined with silicone paper, leave to cool and then crush.

6 To assemble the dish, carefully unwrap one cheesecake from its acetate mould. Cut into 3 sections with two 10cm-long pieces and one of 5cm, and position on a large serving plate. Cover the shorter piece with some of the crushed hazelnuts and spike one of the others with some shards of brittle. Repeat with the remaining three cheesecakes.

7 Whisk the caramel with a hand blender for 3–4 minutes or until you have created a foam. Leave to condense for 1 minute while you finish decorating the plates with small spots of yogurt and the mint leaves. Add the foam and serve immediately.

'The wow of this recipe is in the freshness, the combination of the chocolate and peppermint flavours and the presentation.'

STEPHEN TERRY
THE HARDWICK

Many chefs claim to have been inspired by Marco Pierre White's book *White Heat*, but Stephen Terry had first-hand experience. Aged 21, he worked at Harvey's (alongside a young Gordon Ramsay) and White was 'a significant influence who taught me as much about life as cooking'.

The Good Food Guide first spotted Terry at The Canteen in Chelsea, but it was as head chef at Oliver Peyton's Mayfair restaurant, Coast, that he really made his name – in a kitchen that nurtured a number of rising stars of the future, including Jason Atherton and Mark Sargeant. But, after 20 years of working in some of the most influential kitchens in London, Terry returned to his south Wales roots in 2006 to open The Hardwick. His commitment to local sourcing subsequently gained him the award for Best Use of Local Produce in *The Good Food Guide 2009*, something Stephen Terry puts down to the fact that 'I have learned to appreciate, respect and value produce more than ever and I firmly believe that less is more.'

The perfect setting
Stephen Terry opened The Hardwick in Abergavenny in 2006. Set against a backdrop of the Black Mountains, it's a modest place with quarry tile floors and reclaimed wooden furniture. It is also a pub where simply cooked seasonal produce governs the menu in Italian-inspired dishes such as loin of Welsh pedigree pork served with white polenta, Gorgonzola, bruschetta with cavolo nero and roast chicory.

The Hardwick I Old Raglan Road, Abergavenny, Gwent NP7 9AA
(01873) 854220 I **www.thehardwick.co.uk**

THE HARDWICK

DUM VIVIMUS VIVAMUS

'I may be getting greyer, fatter and more cynical by the day, but age is a good thing. Experience and confidence combined have helped to shape me along my journey.'

Rice pudding with apple compote and shortbread crumble

Stephen Terry

MAKES 4–6 INDIVIDUAL CRUMBLES

FOR THE RICE PUDDING
250ml double cream
250ml milk
1 vanilla pod, split in half lengthways
85g pudding rice
55g caster sugar

FOR THE APPLE COMPOTE
2 large Bramley apples, peeled, cored and cut into 5mm dice
50g caster sugar

FOR THE SHORTBREAD CRUMBLE
25g butter, softened
40g strong white flour
Generous ½ tbsp cornflour
Pinch of baking powder
20g caster sugar
Pinch of Halen Môn sea salt

1 For the rice pudding, put the cream, milk and vanilla pod into a saucepan and slowly bring to the boil. Then add the pudding rice, reduce the heat and simmer for 12–15 minutes or until the rice is just cooked. Add the caster sugar and bring back up to the boil. Remove from the heat, leave to cool and remove the vanilla pod.

2 To make the apple compote, put the apples and caster sugar into a pan and cook over a medium heat until the apples are cooked and tender, but still holding their shape. Remove from the heat and leave to cool.

3 For the crumble, preheat the oven to 140°C/Gas 1. Put all the ingredients in a bowl and rub together with your fingertips to the consistency of large breadcrumbs and then spread on a baking sheet. Cook for about 35 minutes or until golden. Remove and leave to cool.

4 To serve, heat the rice pudding and apple separately. Put the rice pudding and the apple compote in large glasses in alternate layers and sprinkle generously with the shortbread crumble.

'It works so well because the words "rice pudding", "apple", "shortbread" and "crumble" are familiar and comforting. The presentation is where we can make it a little more interesting.'

'Our kitchen garden has taken ten years to get right, but we are now pleasingly proficient and customers really enjoy walking around and seeing produce growing that will be used in the kitchen.'

DAVID PITCHFORD
READ'S

'David Pitchford is thought, in some circles, to be one of the finest chefs in the southeast of England,' stated *The Good Food Guide 1986*, the first year Read's appeared in the Guide. Twenty-five years on and that statement still holds true, with the elegant Georgian manor house on the outskirts of Faversham (to which Read's moved in 2001) home to one of the most renowned fine-dining restaurants in the Home Counties.

Backed by a CV made of solid stuff, including seven years at The Dorchester, David and his wife Rona bought the original Read's 'rather naively' in the inflationary 1970s and went on to establish the restaurant as one of the first in the UK to fly the flag for local produce. That commitment to quality produce prepared with sensitivity remains undimmed: this most unassuming of chefs has never lost the enthusiasm for ingredients as simple as brioche and raspberries combined in a carefully composed dish (see overleaf) that retains a grounding in culinary tradition.

As one of the longest-running husband-and-wife teams in the Guide, the Pitchfords display a mix of creativity and solid management skills and have perfected a personable, unceremonious approach that has delighted a generation of visitors.

Read's | Macknade Manor, Canterbury Road, Faversham, Kent ME13 8XE
(01795) 535344 | **www.reads.com**

Brioche and raspberry pudding
David Pitchford

MAKES 6 INDIVIDUAL PUDDINGS

2 brioche loaves, cut into slices and then into triangles

Butter for the bread

280g fresh or defrosted frozen raspberries

425ml milk

425ml double cream

1 vanilla pod, split in half lengthways

5 eggs

150g caster sugar

TO DECORATE

Icing sugar

18–24 fresh raspberries

Mint leaves

TO SERVE

Double or clotted cream

Specific equipment: see page 259

1 Thinly spread the brioche slices with butter. Lightly grease six 200ml ovenproof dishes and sprinkle with the raspberries. Arrange the brioche slices neatly over the raspberries.

2 Meanwhile, put the milk, cream and vanilla pod into a saucepan and gently heat to simmering point. Beat the eggs and sugar in a large bowl, then whisk in the milk and cream mixture. Strain the custard through a fine sieve.

3 Preheat the oven to 160°C/Gas 3. Put the prepared dishes into a baking tray and pour the custard into each one until full, making sure the brioche slices are well covered or they will burn when cooking. Add hot water to the baking tray and cook in the oven for 20–30 minutes or until set and lightly golden on top.

4 Sprinkle with icing sugar and decorate with 3–4 raspberries (although the dish works well with frozen raspberries inside, they must be fresh on top) and mint leaves. Serve with a jug of double or clotted cream.

'I came up with the idea 25 years ago. Messing around with variations on bread and butter pudding, I discovered that brioche and raspberries worked really well together.'

'Cooking is my passion. I don't do anything else but cook.'

MARY ANN GILCHRIST
CARLTON RIVERSIDE

Chefs don't come more fanatical about cooking and produce than Mary Ann Gilchrist. Her regularly changing menus reflect an insatiable appetite for ideas, irrespective of provenance. Indeed, a 600-strong (and growing) recipe-book collection gives her the inspiration for ways of using the top-quality ingredients that come from a well-established network of suppliers.

For such an instinctive cook, it comes as no surprise that Gilchrist entered the profession by accident – stepping in when the chef walked out of the wine bar/pizzeria she managed in Oxford. It's been quite a journey: from a pub in north Oxfordshire, via a hotel in south Devon to this, the second of her restaurants-with-rooms in Llanwrtyd Wells (she moved from the long-running Carlton House to this attractive riverside property across the road in 2007). Throughout, Gilchrist has built up a loyal following for her clean, simple cooking. Very much the *grande dame* of the Welsh restaurant scene, she believes that it is crucially important that food should taste of what it is and can't stress enough how important it is to source local produce – in fact, 'seasonal' and 'local' are her buzzwords.

Carlton Riverside | Irfon Crescent, Llanwrtyd Wells, Powys LD5 4ST
(01591) 610248 | **www.carltonriverside.com**

Sticky toffee pudding
Mary Ann Gilchrist

MAKES 6 INDIVIDUAL PUDDINGS

100g dates, pitted and chopped
100g butter
100g caster sugar
2 eggs
100g self-raising flour, sifted
Scant tsp bicarbonate of soda

FOR THE STICKY TOFFEE SAUCE

400ml double cream
1½ tbsp black treacle
300g dark soft brown sugar

Specific equipment: see page 259

1 Preheat the oven to 180°C/Gas 4 and grease and flour six 150ml dariole moulds. Put the dates and 200ml of water into a saucepan and bring to the boil. Lower the heat and simmer the dates for a further 10 minutes or until soft.

2 While the dates are simmering, put the butter and sugar into an electric mixer and whisk until they are creamy. Add the eggs one by one, whisking between additions, and then whisk the flour into the mix. Add the bicarbonate of soda to the dates and then add this mixture to the creamed ingredients.

3 Divide the mixture between the moulds and bake in the oven for about 30 minutes or until risen and set. Allow to cool slightly.

4 Meanwhile, make the sticky toffee sauce. Mix together the ingredients in a pan over a high heat and stir until the sugar has dissolved. Bring to the boil, then remove the pan from the heat.

5 Turn the puddings onto individual plates. Pour some of the sauce over the top of each pudding and serve immediately. Serve the remaining sauce separately so your guests can help themselves to more.

'These are intensely light and fluffy, they barely touch your lips and they work really well with the rich, thick, creamy toffee sauce.'

TOM KERRIDGE
THE HAND & FLOWERS

When the Gloucester-born chef opened his own pub in March 2005, it was quite a surprise. With cheffing skills honed in London with leading lights Stephen Bull and Gary Rhodes, and a name made as head chef of the much-acclaimed Adlards in Norwich, he had been expected to take a different route.

The slow pace of Norfolk life had not suited Tom Kerridge, but a chance meal at a top gastropub in Gloucestershire upset plans to return to London. Knocked out by the food, informality and the fact you don't need as much capital setting up in a pub as you do in a restaurant, Kerridge spent a year looking for the right place. The result is The Hand & Flowers, which Kerridge and his wife Beth, who has an artist's eye for design, have together created. It is the blueprint for the perfect pub-with-rooms – and is one of the highest-rated pubs in *The Good Food Guide*.

In good company
Although firmly rooted in the Anglo-French cooking of his early mentors and with a passion for fresh ingredients simply prepared, Kerridge enjoys getting together with chefs whose cooking has taken other directions, such as Simon Rogan, Sat Bains, Claude Bosi and Daniel Clifford. It keeps him motivated and inspired to drive his cooking further and explains the thinking behind his apple crumble soufflé (see overleaf).

The Hand & Flowers | 126 West Street, Marlow, Buckinghamshire SL7 2BP
(01628) 482277 | **www.thehandandflowers.co.uk**

'Installing a new kitchen in November 2008 enabled me to take my cooking a step further. The apple crumble soufflé is an example of this.'

Apple crumble soufflé
Tom Kerridge

MAKES 4–6 INDIVIDUAL SOUFFLÉS

FOR THE FRUIT REDUCTION
250ml Cox apple purée
40g caster sugar
10g cornflour

FOR THE CRÈME PATISSIÈRE
200ml milk
½ vanilla pod, seeds discarded
1 egg
35g caster sugar
20g plain flour
5g cornflour

FOR THE APPLE SORBET
500ml Cox apple juice
100g caster sugar
50g glucose

FOR THE CRUMBLE
75g plain flour
65g caster sugar
30g butter

FOR THE MERINGUE
6 egg whites
2 heaped tbsp caster sugar

FOR THE APPLE PURÉE
2 apples, peeled, cored and chopped
50g caster sugar

FOR THE SOUFFLÉS
1 Cox apple, peeled, cored and diced

**Specific equipment:
see page 259**

1 To make the fruit reduction, whisk together the apple purée and caster sugar in a saucepan and then simmer over a medium heat until reduced by half. Mix the cornflour with a little water to form a paste and add to the purée. Increase the heat to high and cook the purée until it has thickened. Transfer to a food processor and blend, then strain and leave to cool.

2 For the crème patissière, put the milk and vanilla pod in a saucepan and slowly bring to the boil. Meanwhile, beat the egg in a large bowl and then, continuously whisking with a hand-held electric mixer, slowly add the caster sugar, then the flour and, finally, the cornflour. Once the milk has come to the boil, pour it onto the egg custard, mix and whisk. Transfer back to the pan and cook on a medium-high heat for 5–8 minutes or until thick. Pass it through a fine sieve.

3 For the sorbet, bring the apple juice to the boil with 150ml of water in a saucepan. Whisk the sugar and glucose into the juice, bring back up to the boil and then strain through a sieve. Allow to cool and freeze in an ice-cream machine according to the manufacturer's instructions.

4 For the crumble, preheat the oven to 160°C/Gas 3. Rub the flour, sugar and butter together in a bowl to form breadcrumbs, then spread on a baking tray and cook in the oven, stirring every 5 minutes, for 20–25 minutes or until golden. Remove from the oven, leave to cool and then blend in a food processor. Increase the oven temperature to 180°C/Gas 4.

5 Make the meringue by whisking together the egg whites and caster sugar in a bowl to stiff peaks.

6 To make the apple purée, slowly cook the apples and sugar together with 50ml of water in a saucepan for 5–10 minutes or until the apple turns to mush. Pass through a sieve, watering it down if it seems a little thick, and keep warm.

7 To make the soufflés, butter four to six 275ml moulds then quickly swirl sugar around the moulds so that it adheres to the butter. Mix 240g of the fruit reduction with 320g of the crème patissière. Then gently fold in half of the meringue mix, followed by the rest of the meringue. Add 1 tbsp of the crumble and 1 tbsp of the diced Cox apples.

8 Spoon the mix into the moulds, sprinkle more crumble on top and cook in the oven for about 10 minutes or until risen and golden.

9 Serve the soufflés immediately, scattered with some more of the crumble, together with a jug of warm apple purée and a scoop of Cox apple sorbet resting on a bed of crumble.

Glossary

Acetate sheet: More commonly used for overhead projections and presentations, these make a useful tool in the kitchen because of their flexibility. Available at good stationery shops.

Bain marie: Also known as a double boiler, this is a large pan of water above which smaller pans or bowls can be placed so they heat and cook gently. A bain marie is particularly useful for melting chocolate.

Beignet: The French name for a doughnut, the term is used for various types of fried dough, tempura (see entry) and fritter.

Beurre noisette: Literally meaning hazelnut butter, this is butter that has been gently heated until it separates. The milk solids at the bottom begin to turn nut-coloured and smell sweet.

Blanch: To cook briefly in boiling water. Vegetables are generally blanched in plenty of salted water, which allows them to keep their vivid colour as well as a little bite. Meats are also often blanched in unsalted water to remove the strongest flavours and impurities.

Blow torch: Blow torches have a place in kitchens on account of their instant, directable heat. Among other uses, they are ideal for caramelising the sugar topping on crèmes brulées and for heating moulds to turn out jellies and mousses. Domestic versions can be bought in any good cook shop.

Bouillon: The French term for stock, bouillon is generally boiling water flavoured with diced vegetables and herbs that is used to poach fish or meat.

Caramelise: To cook sugar until it turns golden and then brown. Be careful not to go too far, because the sweet rich flavour of caramel can easily turn into a bitter burned taste.

Carpaccio: Very thinly sliced meat or fish and occasionally vegetables and fruit, that is eaten raw.

Chinois: A fine conical sieve.

Clarified butter: Clear butter without milk solids. To clarify butter, melt gently and leave to separate. Pour or ladle off the clear yellow liquid, leaving the solids behind.

Compote: Fruit that has been stewed or cooked in syrup – the texture should be rough rather than smooth.

Confit: A traditional way of preserving ingredients through very slow cooking. For savoury ingredients, the process usually involves cooking in goose or duck fat, though it can be used to describe a slow cooking in sugar, for example for fruit.

Cream whipper: A device similar to a soda siphon that produces perfectly whipped cream (or similar liquids) in an instant by the addition of carbon dioxide. Available in some good cook shops and online.

Deep-fat fryer: An appliance that has a basket for raising food clear of the oil when the cooking is complete.

Deglaze: The object of deglazing is to melt the evaporated juices left on the cooking pan to use them and their flavours in a sauce. To deglaze, pour off excess fat or oil and then add liquid (usually alcohol, stock or water) to the hot pan, scraping the caramelised juices to help dissolve them.

Drum sieve: A drum-shaped fine sieve, also known as a tamis. Usually used for sieving flour, because it has a flat surface, a drum sieve is also very useful for rubbing processed meat or fish through, to make sure there is no sinew in the finished product.

Galette: French for a type of pancake or large flat cake.

Ganache: Normally a chocolate coating or filling, it can be adapted with different flavours, such as banana.

Gremolata: A seasoning made of grated citrus, parsley and garlic that is sprinkled onto fish, pasta or meat just before serving.

Ice-cream machine: An appliance with a bowl that is frozen and which then freezes the ice cream mixture with the help of a motor. This turns the bowl or a paddle inserted into the top, making ice cream in 15–30 minutes.

Isomalt: A sugar substitute that contains 50 per cent fewer calories than sugar and is much easier to work with than ordinary sugar when making decorations. Available at good kitchen shops and online.

Joconde sponge: A rich but light almond sponge, which is widely used in constructed desserts.

Liquid nitrogen: Nitrogen gas chilled to a very low temperature (−196°C) so that it resembles a water-like liquid. Used to chill dishes and components of dishes very quickly to a deep, deep freeze.

Mandoline: A slicer used to cut vegetables into wafer-thin slices.

Meringue, ribbon stage: When meringue is whipped so the egg white forms a thick white ribbon from the whisk to the bowl when the whisk is lifted gently.

Meringue, soft peak stage: When meringue is whipped so the mixture sits in soft white peaks when the whisk is removed (a few more turns than the ribbon stage).

Micro herbs: Very young herbs with tiny leaves, these herbs look beautiful as a garnish and have an intense flavour. Available at specialist greengrocers, or grow your own.

Mousseline: A sauce that is given lightness by the addition of whipped cream. It can be sweet or savoury, but will always be light and refined.

Parfait: A cold, sweet or savoury mousse that is made either by mixing and freezing ingredients together or by using gelatine to set them together, or a combination of the two.

Quenelle: A scoop of mixture formed with two spoons. It can be a mousse that is then poached in boiling water to set or it can be an ice cream, sorbet or cream mixture.

Reduce: To reduce a sauce, bring the contents of the saucepan to the boil and leave until the liquid inside has reduced to the specified amount. This intensifies the flavours of the liquid left behind.

Remoulade: A mayonnaise-like sauce that is traditionally served with matchsticks of raw celeriac to make celeriac remoulade.

Romesco sauce: A traditional sauce from Tarragona in Catalonia, Spain. It is based on almonds, peppers and tomatoes and can be used to accompany grilled and barbecued dishes. It also works well with full-flavoured roast game.

Sabayon: A light frothy sauce that is made by whipping egg yolks as they cook gently, adding flavourings at the same time. A sabayon is traditionally sweet, but adapts well to incorporate savoury flavours.

Silicone paper: Also known as silicone sheets or mats, these flexible, non-stick baking sheets can be heated to very high temperatures and chilled to very low temperatures, and can be reused again and again. Available in cook shops and supermarkets.

Sous vide bag: The French name for a plastic bag that can be sealed without air in it (vacuum pack or vac-pack). A good substitute at home is a transparent roaster bag large enough to be tied up once the air has been pushed out and then knotted to keep the water away from whatever is cooking inside.

Sweat: Cook gently in butter or oil (or both) over a low heat and with a lid on so the vegetables (most usually onion and garlic) gain a translucency without browning.

Tempura batter: A light, originally Japanese, batter that is used for deep-frying fish and vegetables to give a beautifully crunchy exterior.

Thermometer: Cooking thermometers are available in various dial or digital versions. Different thermometers do different jobs, such as for cooking meat or to check the heat of jam, sugar or chips.

Velouté: A rich velvet-like sauce, made by ingredients that have been reduced to intensify the flavours and a white roux or cream added for thickening.

Wet garlic: Sweet fresh garlic, rather than the stored variety usually found in the kitchen. Fresh garlic has long green leaves, but with the distinctive garlic bulb at the base. The smell is much more vibrant and the taste is less harsh when garlic is fresh. Garlic is in season in the spring and early summer months.

Specific equipment

We realise that some of the equipment specified in the recipes is not readily available in the average domestic kitchen. For ease, we have therefore listed below the recipes that require specific equipment – although this is by no means comprehensive and we would recommend that you read a recipe thoroughly to make sure you have all the materials to hand. Of course, one person's kitchen godsend may be unfamiliar to another. So do also use the adjacent glossary, which explains what many of the tools involve and where you can buy the more unusual items.

Page 24
Sous vide bag, water bath and ice bath (optional)
Cream whipper (optional)
Liquid nitrogen

Page 28
Four 80ml china moulds or ramekins
Sandwich maker or panini machine

Page 48
Pasta machine
Four 6cm-diameter x 4.5cm-deep metal rings

Page 60
Pasta machine
7cm- and 6cm-diameter cutters
Sous vide bag

Page 72
Sous vide bag or microwave fish bags

Page 88
15 x 8 x 8cm terrine mould

Page 98
Cream whipper (optional)

Page 158
Pasta machine (optional)

Page 170
Six 500ml pie dishes

Page 184
Four 7.5cm-diameter x 5cm-deep (about 150ml) dariole moulds

Page 192
Blow torch
c. 15 x 11cm shallow container

Page 196
c. 15 x 20cm shallow container
Blow torch

Page 200
Blow torch
Egg-top remover (optional)

Page 204
23cm-diameter cake tin
7cm-diameter cutter

Page 208
23 x 18 x 4cm baking tray

Page 212
23 x 18 x 4cm baking tray
10 x 10cm metal frame

Page 216
Four 125ml crème caramel or dariole moulds or ramekins

Page 224
Four 5cm-diameter half-sphere moulds
Four 5cm-diameter hexagonal moulds
23 x 18 x 4cm baking tray
Chocolate spray gun
Blow torch

Page 228
Eight 10cm-diameter, loose-bottomed cake tins

Page 236
15 x 9cm shallow container
20 x 7cm shallow container
Sheets of acetate
2cm-diameter cutter

Page 240
Sheets of acetate

Page 248
Six 200ml ovenproof dishes

Page 252
Six 150ml dariole moulds

Page 256
Four to six 275ml moulds

Index

Main entries for chefs and restaurants are in **bold**

Acknowledgements

The publishers would like to thank the following people for helping to create this book: Kirstie Addis, Francesca Bashall, Ian Brereton, Emma Callery, Elizabeth Carter, Margaret Clancy, Katy Denny, Nikki English, Alix Godfree, Lisa Grey, Amy Hart, Jonathan Hedley, Ben Kay, Angela Newton, Kate Parker, Jurgita Sirvydyte, Peter Smith, Emma Sturgess, Mark Taylor, Yehrin Tong, Stuart Walton and Blânche Williams.

The publishers would like to thank the following for their photographs: p9 Rosie Hallam; pp42 and 45 Jason Lowe; pp50–3 Myburgh Du Plessis; pp66–9 Alan Donaldson; p163 © Quentin Bacon/Gordon Ramsay; pp182–5 Marc Millar; p189 © Lisa Barber at www.lisabarber.co.uk; p218 Philip Hollis; p219 top right and middle right David Loftus; pp250–3 Steve France. All other photographs are © Which? Ltd with the exception of those on the following pages, which have been licensed for use: 22, 25, 26–9, 30–3, 34–7, 46–9, 54–7, 62–3, 70–3, 82–5, 86–9, 90, 100–103, 221, 132, 136–9, 140–3, 144, 148–9, 152–5, 156–9, 160–1, 164–7, 190–3, 222–5, 226–9, 231, 247.

The following recipes are reproduced with the kind permission of: p44 Fried duck's egg with sprue asparagus and brown shrimps/Mark Hix from *HIX Oyster and Chop House* published by Quadrille; p150 Roast woodcock with grapes and marc/Michel Roux Jr from *Le Gavroche Cookbook* © Michel Roux Jr. 2001, published by Weidenfeld & Nicolson, an imprint of The Orion Publishing Group, London; p162 Roasted loin of venison with braised red cabbage, parsnip chips and parsnip purée/Gordon Ramsay from *Three Star Chef* published by Quadrille; p188 Sorrel ice cream with wood sorrel and compote of brambles from *Dessert: Recipes from Le Champignon Sauvage* by David Everitt-Matthias (Absolute Press, 2009).